Francis Ford Coppola |

Contemporary Film Directors

Edited by Justus Nieland and Jennifer Fay

The Contemporary Film Directors series provides concise, well-written introductions to directors from around the world and from every level of the film industry. Its chief aims are to broaden our awareness of important artists, to give serious critical attention to their work, and to illustrate the variety and vitality of contemporary cinema. Contributors to the series include an array of internationally respected critics and academics. Each volume contains an incisive critical commentary, an informative interview with the director, and a detailed filmography.

A list of books in the series appears
at the end of this book.

Francis Ford Coppola |

Jeff Menne

**UNIVERSITY
OF
ILLINOIS PRESS**
URBANA,
CHICAGO,
AND
SPRINGFIELD

Frontispiece: Francis Ford Coppola and his daughter, Sofia,
on the set of *The Godfather, Part II.*

Library of Congress Cataloging-in-Publication Data
Menne, Jeff, 1974–
Francis Ford Coppola / by Jeff Menne.
pages   cm. — (Contemporary film directors)
Includes bibliographical references and index.
Includes filmography.
ISBN 978-0-252-03882-2 (hardcover : alk. paper) —
ISBN 978-0-252-08037-1 (pbk. : alk. paper) —
ISBN 978-0-252-09678-5 (e-book)
1. Coppola, Francis Ford, 1939– —Criticism and interpretation. I. Title.
PN1998.3.C67M36   2014
791.4302'33092—dc23   2014018098

Contents |

Acknowledgments | ix

FRANCIS FORD COPPOLA
AND THE UNDERGROUND CORPORATION | 1

Is the Ford in John Ford the Ford
in Francis Ford Coppola? 10

The Cinema of Finance Capital 15

Hippies, Inc: *The Rain People*
and the Making of American Zoetrope 23

The Form of the Firm: *The Godfather,
The Conversation,* and *Tucker* 42

Family Capital 52

The Paranoid Style in Corporate History 59

Grounding the Corporation 67

Vocal Apparitions and Corporate Personhood:
Apocalypse Now, The Godfather, Part III, and *Tetro* 76

Mechanized Family 90

Zoetrope Postmodernism
and the Amazing Technicolor Family 100

INTERVIEW WITH FRANCIS FORD COPPOLA | 123

Filmography | 129

Bibliography | 141

Index | 145

Acknowledgments |

This material went from being a small part of a larger project to a book all its own thanks to Jennifer Fay, who encouraged it in germinal form and helped it along with smart readings at each stage in its development. She is a brilliant reader, and a deeply generous scholar. It was my great luck, then, to have feedback on this high order from a series of readers. Justus Nieland, I should note in particular, gave wonderful conceptual responses to the project, and Jon Lewis—whom I have long held to be the best, most innovative Coppola scholar—supported this project, and this gave it instant legitimacy for me. Without his work, I wouldn't have done mine in this way. I am most grateful, as well, to have worked with the editors at Illinois, who were smart and helpful at each turn. Thanks to Danny Nasset, for seeing me through the project, and to Matt Mitchell, for his superb help in copyediting.

My last three years in the Screen Studies program at Oklahoma State University have provided a collegial setting for my research—good conversation, and kind support—and for this research in particular I received an internal grant from the college, and an external grant from the Oklahoma Humanities Council. This enabled my trips to the Margaret Herrick Library and to the Pacific Film Archive. At the latter, Nancy Goldman was especially helpful in making materials available to me. I am grateful for this assistance that proved so vital in realizing this book. But I want to recognize, too, the stray leads given me by Josh Glick and by my research assistants, Clayton Dillard and Jacob Floyd. I thank Francis Ford Coppola most emphatically for granting me an interview.

Finally, I owe the most unpayable debt to my inner circle. To Anne Kuhbander, there are not enough thanks. She understands the gravity of work, and the levity of non-work. Our sons, Owen and Max, make everything take longer, and because I think life should be longer, they seem helpful. I dedicate this book to Melvin Kuhbander, who believed in other people, and I am forever grateful that he believed in me. We talked about this book at its inception; I'm sure he'd be thrilled that it's been accomplished.

Francis Ford Coppola |

Francis Ford Coppola |
and the Underground Corporation

"This playground is no place for permanency."
—Michael Pye and Lynda Myles, *The Movie Brats*

Because in most accounts Francis Ford Coppola is a governing force
behind the New Hollywood, it seems that people can't help referring
to him as the "Godfather," whether it's to recognize his patronage (his
associate John Korty calls him "the impresario, essentially the Godfather"), or the network formed around him (Steven Bach calls Coppola,
George Lucas, Walter Murch, and others the "Mill Valley Mafia"), or
even his personal manner (a *Vanity Fair* profile likened him to one of
his onscreen Mafia dons).[1] The term suggests itself, such is the strong
identity in the public mind between him and his famous movie franchise.
If the term is anything more than cliché, it might illuminate the extent
to which Coppola has been the maker of his own informal economy.
This economy, we might say, is a shadow economy of Hollywood, where
once moviemaking had been arranged like clockwork.

   "Clockwork" describes not only the production rate of the Old Hollywood studio system, where the integrated majors had turned out movies
one a week, but the U.S. economy in general, as throughout the first half

of the twentieth century it fell under the sway of scientific management. In production of this kind, labor was treated in terms of quantity, not quality. Hollywood movies might protest this, as did *Modern Times* (dir. Charlie Chaplin, 1936), which opens on the image of a clock face and shows the laboring Little Tramp dominated by its accelerated tempo; but Hollywood was itself known, often in the person of Irving Thalberg, for cutting its production process to this measure. Placing the creative labor of moviemaking on the same foundations as any manufacture, though, had a twofold effect of rendering the movies suspicious as an art form, because they were too much an industry, and of forcing would-be advocates of the seventh art into curious theoretical defenses against its industrial character. "The only great films to come out of Hollywood," claimed the postwar intellectual Dwight Macdonald, "were made before industrial elelphantiasis had reduced the director to one of a number of technicians all operating at about the same level of authority."[2] The great directors, for Macdonald, were "Griffith and Stroheim," since they were able to make movies before investment banking had made their art so capital-intensive that the efficiency movement had to take note.[3] When it did, Stroheim famously had his wings clipped by management-minded Irving Thalberg.[4]

Macdonald's view is instructive, in that its reworking as the "auteur theory" would let those coming of age in the 1960s cast the terms of art and industry in more complex relationship. If, for instance, film became art only by fully vesting authority in the director—as "was so in the pre-1930 cinema," according to Macdonald—then any theory of film art applied to Hollywood might also double as a theory of its industrial reorganization.[5] This was true of auteur theory, I argue, as its main tenet—that certain Hollywood directors had sensibilities bold enough to neutralize industrial hierarchy in the name of creativity and self-expression—turned out to have similar prescriptive force in postwar business culture. Hosannas to unruly sensibility, though in cultural memory they belong to the counterculture, arose too in a business world wishing itself rid of a company-man ethos.[6] In short, business wasn't scandalized by the 1960s and the style of the counterculture; it learned from it. The entrepreneurial culture that became the basis of the New Economy bears much of the counterculture within it.[7]

Francis Ford Coppola's career should be understood in this context. Taking a page from his mentor Roger Corman—who "had a great knack," it's said, "for finding talented people who were willing to work for practically nothing"—Coppola gathered his film-school friends to form American Zoetrope, an off-Hollywood production firm that, like American International Pictures (AIP) before it, would make its way by setting up operations beyond the reach of the regulatory controls that had frozen young talent out of Hollywood.[8] Unlike AIP, though, American Zoetrope was underwritten by a Hollywood studio. When the return on investment of *Easy Rider* (dir. Dennis Hopper, 1969) suggested to studio Hollywood that there was money it didn't know how to make, and that there were audiences that it didn't know existed, Warner Bros. turned to Coppola because, as John Milius jokes, he had "a beard" and knew "hippies."[9] Coppola chose San Francisco for Zoetrope's base, indeed, because it was an epicenter of the counterculture, and he wanted "bohemian life," he says, to pervade the corporation.[10] And it did. Its brash colors showed in the décor of Zoetrope's Fulton Street headquarters, and its celebrities—Jerry Garcia, Bill Graham (the concert promoter), and others—were drawn to Zoetrope as a center of gravity. "It was all extremely exciting," Walter Murch says, Zoetrope for him being "a professional extension of the film school ideal."[11]

However, what kept Zoetrope from being another experiment for what Fred Turner calls the New Communalists, common enough then in and around San Francisco, was that the device organizing the endeavors of these like-minded friends was the corporation.[12] They bent the device to their own ends, no doubt, but the effect was that corporate form partook of the informal energies on which the art world runs. Contrary, then, to many film historians who place American Zoetrope outside the bailiwick of Hollywood commerce, as a short-lived refuge for film art, I see it as an agent of renewal in corporate history for the way it formed a micro-economy—a place apart, with codes all its own—that nested inside the economies of scale of the conglomerated corporations.

Coppola has shown an unusually sophisticated sense of the part he had in economy and that it had in him, and not only in his initiative to self-operate through Zoetrope. His movies read as declarations of New Economy, as chances to allegorize in film form the social relations that have permitted their making. Consider the final scenes of *Tucker* (1988), which use the same technique of parallel montage on display in the climax of *The Godfather* (1972). In *The Godfather*, we see Michael Corleone's (Al Pacino) power consolidated by way of intercut images of his baptismal observance and his authorized murders. In one set of images, Michael says vows as his nephew is baptized into the church; in the other, his henchmen kill rival mob bosses so that power is Michael's alone. The tension lays between his public standing in the community and the behind-the-scenes machinations that underwrite it. In *Tucker*, however, while we find dirty work hidden behind the rituals of community life, it is of a different sort. There, we watch Preston Tucker (Jeff Bridges) stand trial for alleged fraud, but as he is detained in the courtroom, the workforce of Tucker Motor Company is at his factory assembling the last several cars that they are accused of having no intention to build. The tension, once more, gathers in the mismatch between professed norms and actual practices. Hypocrisy is the effect produced by the crosscutting technique in both movies.

But in *The Godfather*, if it seems hypocritical that Michael denounces Satan's work inside the church but executes it outside its walls, it's a hypocrisy that everyone has fully internalized. Connie knows the price of her family's power. The community accepts their don's protection. Theirs is a polity within the larger polity, and informal law is all they can institute for themselves. Kay cannot live with the hypocrisy, of course, because as an East Coast WASP she enjoys full membership in the larger polity and need not find recourse in the informal law of the smaller, ghettoized polity. In *Tucker* it is much different. The hypocrisy is not that Preston Tucker says one thing in the courtroom, for show, but then does the opposite on his personal time. He says the exact same thing in both circumstances. What first strikes the viewer as hypocritical, rather, is a national ideology that exalts a man like Tucker, a rugged individual, while a federal court is stacked against the actual flesh-and-blood Tucker by the Big Three automakers and the politicians effectively on their payroll.

Despite producer George Lucas's wish that the movie have a Capra feel, with a little guy taking on a corrupt system, *Tucker* is a story of another kind. What we see in the Tucker factory cuts against our nor-

In *The Godfather,* Michael stands as the godfather at his nephew's baptism . . .

. . . while his henchmen, at his bidding, assassinate rival mafia bosses.

mative view of labor: four men throwing in together, working around the clock not for overtime but *for no pay at all,* the work issuing from their hands rather than specialized machines—they present an image of heroic labor, as it were, a holdover from an age of proud craftspeople. Their work is motivated by love, not by baser incentives. "Won't be the first time we've worked for free," one employee jokes. On meeting their contractual quota, they embrace each other and toast champagne. This is not a lone instance of alcohol on the shop floor, as beer-drinking has been part of their work culture. And not as contraband, for no line divides licit and illicit work behavior other than the one they themselves decide to draw.

It's not even clear where the borders of the shop floor might lie. Tucker has built his workshop, the Ypsilanti Tool and Machine Company, a stone's throw from his home. When asked to describe the company's factory, a witness replies, "What factory? It's a barn." The prosecution claims that for Tucker's engine, "most of the work had to be done on a kitchen stove." These claims, they believe, prove that Tucker did not carry out his work with serious intent. The only proof of that, though, would be a poorly made car, or no car at all, but the *coup de grâce* for the defense is that a fleet of stylish, roadworthy Tucker 48's has been parked curbside outside the courtroom windows. What the prosecution has proven, instead, is that a premium car has been produced by labor unregulated by the juridical standards of the land. Seeing the ineluctability of this logic—namely, that labor might self-organize, without any intervention from the state—the prosecution can only assert the nonexistence of Tucker's cars. There is physical evidence for their existence, of course, and it lies in plain view of the jury. But it cannot constitute juridical proof: the cars are inadmissible in the hearings, for reasons the plot leaves unclear. Once acquitted, Tucker baits the court by inviting the jury to "take a ride in one of those Tucker cars that don't exist."

Willed blindness of this kind typifies informal economy as a concept, Manuel Castells and Alejandro Portes say, noting Spain's practice of exporting "millions of dollars worth of shoes and other articles produced in factories that do not legally exist."[13] The hypocrisy, if we should stick with that term, is that formal law cannot recognize the growing presence of an informal economy that threatens to upset all it had held in place. Such recognition, in particular, would throw into crisis what is known as the "liberal consensus," the Keynesian détente that had been struck between business and labor, with the state its mediator. This equilibrium was considered the great, if volatile, achievement of postwar political economy.

Because the industrial arrangement in place characterized not only the postwar car industry but Hollywood too, it's easy to take *Tucker* as Coppola's midcareer reckoning with the conditions in Hollywood as he once found them, then changed them, and now experiences them once more—again as oppressive—in the wake of his changes. Latter-day critics tell the story of Coppola's entry into the industry as if he were some striding colossus—"the rebel envoy," as John Milius called him, in "the walled city."[14] The hagiography of Coppola, and others in his generation, was prepared by the auteur theory, the critical approach Andrew Sarris adapted from the French New Wave that suggested that any Hollywood (i.e. mass-produced) art must come from "a few brave spirits" who have "miraculously extracted" it from their "money-oriented environment."[15] But *Tucker* undoes the simplistic dyad of individual *contra* industry that had given auteur theory its broad appeal. It is the group spirit, finally, that compensates Tucker's individual failings ("He just doesn't understand how a corporation runs," says a board member, "and he's not much of an engineer, either") and lets the Tucker company realize their prototype design. The men in the plant build the car, after all, while Tucker is a courtroom spectacle; this is what the cross-cutting has told us. Coppola himself would downplay the auteur theory. "Every element, when you're lucky, comes together," he says of *The Godfather*, recognizing the "wonderful composer," the "great photographer," the production design, and so on. When people ask him what role he had, given all their talents, he responds, "Well, I chose them."[16]

If *Tucker* does not support auteur theory, neither does it dispel it altogether. The movie takes Tucker's name for its title, after all, as does the car his company built, suggesting an essential function left to the individual signature. When a promotional film is being made for the Tucker car, and its filmmaker needs personal footage of Tucker, they explain that in order to sell stock they need to sell Tucker as a person, "an image." This might let us think *Tucker* is but a cynical backward glance at Hollywood's auteur phase: it advertised individual glory, briefly, so its massified audience would more gamely consent to its culture-industry vassalage. This, indeed, is auteur theory understood from the standpoint of circulation. And though any interpretation of *Tucker* needs to make sense of its style, which is clearly a pastiche of gaudy marketing effects, a good-faith reckoning with the movie requires that we consider its interest in the production process. Whatever the downstream fate of goods—the cars that may one day become collector's items, the movies that may one day ride high on American Film Institute lists—this is nothing but the afterlife of production.

In this regard, the movie makes the case, as Coppola will do frequently elsewhere, that auteur theory is a form of business-management theory. Consider several scenes from the movie. When the car designer Alex Tremulis (Elias Koteas) overrides an idea in Tucker's original model, Tucker tells him, "You ever do that again, something I told you not to—so help me, I'll give you a raise." Tucker sought the better idea, the movie insists, no matter where it occurred in the hierarchy. Coppola's modest claim that his role as director is limited to choosing personnel is here complicated by the fact that choosing talent is itself meaningless if one doesn't also construct the environment in which talent might realize itself. Tucker, we see, gets his employees to work at full capacity by spreading his dream of self-realization to them. The site of labor becomes for them the arena for the whole self. This cuts against the doxa of scientific management, a.k.a. Taylorism, which coordinated the total operation of a plant precisely by disaggregating the individual into a set of functions, energies, and skills in order to recombine them at a higher level. Tucker's style, in contrast, sets loose the creative energy in those around him, and leads to the absolute trust of his team. Abe Karatz (Martin Landau) confirms as much when asked under cross-examination if, as an ex-convict, he expects one person to believe what he's saying, and he responds, "One," while locking eyes with Tucker. The corollary to absolute trust, finally, is absolute commitment. When, after working around the clock, Eddie Dean falls asleep in a chair, a coworker rouses him and reminds him of their deadline the next day. The managerial function, we see, has been democratized throughout the shop floor, such that, in essence, the voice of management is one's own.

"Art never sleeps" read a note that Coppola's son, Gio, posted in his workspace.[17] The artist, that is, works overtime. In a real sense, we have to believe that auteur theory—a theory that an artist is reflected in his or her labor, but a technician is not—is the only doctrine suited to realizing the postwar management ambition, most notably proselytized by Douglas McGregor, of making "unimagined resources of creative human energy . . . available within the organizational setting."[18] This, in fact, is how Pauline Kael describes Orson Welles's auteurist achievement, *Citizen Kane* (1941). Kael belittles the need to think of Welles's great work as "the result of a single artistic intelligence" and instead celebrates his ability to break the yoke of Old Hollywood, where "almost everyone worked beneath his capacity," in order to "liberate and utilize the talents of his co-workers."[19] This was Coppola's raison d'être early on. He did not begin his career with a series of dazzling movies. Neither *Dementia 13* (1963), *You're a Big Boy Now* (1966), *Finian's Rainbow* (1968), nor *The Rain People* (1969) would make his name. "It's true," he said then, "that I've never made a successful film."[20] He would soon make *The Godfather*, and then this statement would be spectacularly reversed. But when he admitted that he had "never made a successful film," I shall argue, his chief interest was to make American Zoetrope, a corporate form bringing together a congeries of underground practices that, were they mainstreamed, would spell the end of Old Hollywood. "I don't think there'll be a Hollywood as we know it," Coppola predicted, "when this generation of film students gets out of college."[21]

It is not wrong, therefore, to consider the auteur theory the watershed between Old and New Hollywood, so long as we don't think it signaled the individual's messianic overcoming of the stubbornly profit-minded corporation. What it did, rather less romantically and more efficaciously, was help reconfigure corporate capital. In a telling scene in *Tucker*, when the industrial filmmaker asks Preston Tucker to gaze at the sign atop his manufacturing plant—a photo-op of the man seeing his name in outsize letters—what Tucker should see is himself reflected in corporate enterprise. It is only a reflection, though, for the name does not belong to him but to the firm. In fact, when in real life Tucker later tried designing a new car after he failed to mass-produce the Tucker 48, he could not use his name for it because, legally, he did not own it. He had let it sponsor other projects. In the courtroom he argues just this prerogative (for "Edison, the Wright Brothers, Mr. Ford" as namesake mechanisms of "better idea" production); and in the workplace he puts it into practice, conferring his own name, in perpetuity, on a generative

In a lap dissolve, Preston Tucker fades into insubstantiality behind the more durable brand name, Tucker.

process. This conferral is best understood as the paradoxical work that the auteur theory performed for Hollywood in synchronizing the projects of the individual and of the corporation.

Is the Ford in John Ford the Ford in Francis Ford Coppola?

If Preston Tucker placed himself in a lineage with "Mr. Ford"—or at least Coppola presents it this way, claiming, "We might have *had* a Henry Ford in the forties" and "his name was Preston Tucker"—we might here work out the analogy to include Coppola in its historical logic.[22] It is one of the poetic felicities of Hollywood tradition that the emblematic movie director of the studio era, John Ford, shared a name with the emblematic movie director of the post-studio era, Francis Ford Coppola. The name Ford, we might say, was given these men by the system of which they were a part every bit as much as they (or their parents) might claim to have chosen it of free will. The name was in the air, that is, and it named, ultimately, a system more than a car. The "system" refers generally to the American economic order in which they were reared—none in their generation could be ignorant of Henry Ford, and many performed their daily labor in the style he patented—but it also refers to Hollywood, the system in which culture had been mass-produced on the principles for which Henry Ford was famous.

John Ford would disavow the association. He and his brother changed their last name from Feeney to Ford, and though they disagree on the source of their adopted name, John Ford assured that it was no tribute to the automaker. The irony, of course, is that the Hollywood industry in which John Ford made his career was, during his active years, very much a tribute to Henry Ford and his production model. Nothing was more routine than the production schedules of the Hollywood majors. Some debate surrounds the putative Fordism of classical Hollywood cinema, to be sure, with the sticking point of movies not being precisely standardized sometimes obscuring how centrally Hollywood belonged to the Fordist regime.[23] It is with this in mind—that Hollywood cannot make the same exact movie over and over—that Janet Staiger carries out one of the more thoroughgoing studies of the developing Hollywood mode of production.[24] While Staiger acknowledges that in Hollywood a contest between standardization and differentiation meant that "filmmaking did not achieve the assembly-line uniformity prevalent in other industries," she charts the systematic drift away from craft labor to a detailed division of labor that made Hollywood a "factory system" at home in the "context" of other "concurrent U.S. business practices."[25] In this context, Hollywood industry certainly looked like Fordist manufacture to its contemporaries. *Motography* saw the early Selig plant, for instance, as an "art factory" turning out movies "with the same amount of organized efficiency, division of labor and manipulation of matter as if they were locomotives or sewing machines."[26] It was the management of the work, rather than the results of the work per se, that revealed its essential Fordism. As Hollywood evolved its economies of scale, "System and Efficiency" set in, its insiders would say, such that its total operations could be brought under a "management hierarchy."[27] The sequence that Staiger documents (the director system, the director-unit system, the central producer system, and the producer-unit system) attests to the stages of refinement in Hollywood's commitment to "scientific management."[28]

Pursuing his career within this maturing industry, John Ford not only disavowed his association with Henry Ford, which his brother found unproblematic, but he chose a storytelling idiom, Hollywood's Western, that was interested exclusively in a world of preindustrial labor. Westerns, he confessed, were his "chance to get away from Hollywood," with its "smog" of industry.[29] The aesthetic claim of the genre, in all its imagery of open land, was put on the space that still spread beyond and outside the articulations of Fordism. There, John Ford felt he could do a "job of work."[30] If his movies find a way to narrate the business culture that was home to his everyday labor, it is only by negation: industrialism, which makes everyone subordinate to its system, is replaced by agrarianism, which had room left for sovereign individualism. Or anyway, the agrarian society could be nostalgically recalled this way.

Here the difference between John Ford and Francis Ford Coppola is pointed. The latter director addressed, as squarely as possible, the system in which he worked through the movies it let him make. This is not to say that Coppola thought critically, whereas Ford did not. It's only to say that, for historical reasons, critique would look different for the two directors. The Fordist subject, by design, is deterred from focusing on work close at hand because the goal of this labor system has been to minimize one's work, and hence too one's investment in it, and to remove its total process from view. Even in the grips of Fordism, though, there is critique; it just looks different. When John Ford narrated the unfulfilled project of industrial citizenship, say, in *How Green Was My Valley* (1941), he did so by displacing the problem into a European past. This is because Fordism, when successful, goes cognitively unprocessed. History suggests that it only became available as an object of critique—and this will mark the difference between the Old and New Hollywood, and, the Old and New Left—when Fordism found itself in full-blown crisis.

Beginning his career when he did, Coppola enjoyed a different relationship to Fordism altogether. On April 7, 1939, a few weeks after John Ford released *Stagecoach*, Francis Ford Coppola was born in Detroit, the epicenter of Henry Ford's production methods. His family lived there, somewhat transiently, because his father, Carmine, was flautist of the Detroit Symphony Orchestra. Francis was born in the Henry Ford Hospital, and his names were given him in recognition of his maternal grandfather, Francesco Pennino, and of the sponsor of his father's radio show, *Ford Sunday Evening Hour*.[31] Coppola became famous under that name, which likely means that he'll never be known otherwise. But in 1977 he dropped the middle name, Ford, because he believed no one could trust a "man with three names."[32] Though I have no reason to dispute his explanation, it seems unlikely that Coppola, being so expert at fashioning meaning, would miss the symbolism in his ridding himself of Ford. One might argue, after all, that he did as much for Hollywood. In what follows I will pursue a modest version of such a claim—not that Coppola singlehandedly changed the inner workings of Hollywood, but that he played a part within his own industry, as members of his generation did in other industries, to redefine the labor of individuals that, taken together, makes an economy. Coppola fits next to other such spokespeople—Stewart Brand, say, and later Steve Jobs in the information sector, and before them Betty Friedan in behalf of women debarred from industry—but the antagonist they all had in common was Henry Ford and the ideas that, in his name, had firmly cast the arrangement of labor in public and private life. If from one end of the telescope they look like mavericks, ready to smash the system, from the other end they look like its custodians. The change they exacted in what we might call the "regime of accumulation," Fordist-Keynesianism, had the effect, some say, of unleashing capitalism.[33] Milton Friedman, a Chicago school economist, was happy for this; David Harvey, a Marxist critic, was not. But these individuals who radicalized postwar labor relations could not, it's safe to say, always guess the direction in which history would channel their activism. They moved with the tides of history, though, and this is what gave their efforts such force in the first place. My study hence presumes that the movement beyond Fordism must be seen within two orders of activity: one the vast historical order of global economy, and the other the smaller individual order of local industry.

This book tracks the extent to which Coppola used his movies to make this history intelligible in individualist terms. In them, he coordinated the domains of the private and the public self, removing the partitions that had made one's personal labor seem unrelated to global processes. Coppola's cinema, its theme and variations, aspired after an integrated whole. His canniest insight into Henry Ford, in fact, was that Ford "wasn't just designing cars; in effect, he was designing cities as well."[34] And this would hold true, too, for the studios, which often were literally cities—Universal City, Fox's Movietone City—with assorted municipal services, mayors, police, and so on. Once we recognize the studios as totalized spaces for living, we must in turn treat their management as not only workplace policy but as social philosophy.

In a brilliant analysis of Ford's project, the management theorist Peter Drucker states Coppola's insight in different words: "[M]ass production is not a mechanical principle but a *principle of social organization.*"[35] It gives rise to a society, a city beyond the shop floor, because "it organizes men and their work." The society it creates, Drucker concludes, is one in which the individual is "ineffectual" and "the whole—the organized group—is clearly not only more than, but different from, the sum of its parts."[36] This means that the individual must take itself to be different in substance from a society that it must regard, functionally, as an organism: the total action in mass production, that is, seems no less sophisticated than craft work, and may seem even more so, yet the skill involved—the intelligence, as it were—is commuted "further up the line." The "job," then, "is more skilled" than the people; the valorized "being" must be conceived on a transpersonal order.[37]

This makes for the most intractable conceptual problem in industrial society, which has only yielded the elegant, if largely sophistical, notion of corporate personhood as its solution. But Ford's failure, Drucker says, lay in not fighting this problem nor desiring this solution. He nurtured, instead, the utopian dream of reclaiming the "Jeffersonian society of independent equals." In his factories he tried to solve problems of a bygone order, as it were, by making one's work a matter of neither "skill nor brawn nor mental effort" and hence leaving these faculties "fully available for [one's] community life as an independent Jeffersonian citizen outside of the plant and after working hours."[38] This left a divided society, with "the functional grandeur of the River Rouge Plant" on one side and "the social jungle that is Detroit" on the other side.[39] The root problem of the industrial order had been left, all the while, to multiply in the culture of Ford's plant.

If Coppola has been criticized often for hubris, it is because he believed that he could solve Ford's leftover problem with his firm, American Zoetrope, and that the new city that would flow from it might be conceptually prepared in movie form, with *Megalopolis.* The unmade movie, *Megalopolis,* lagged behind the unrealized firm, American Zoetrope, by twenty years: after *Tucker* wrapped, he began planning it. Of

Megalopolis he has said that the cinema has resources enough to offer "a precise social and architectural rendering" of "the world of the future."[40] Coppola could not build it per se, he thought, not in concrete form; he could, however, build its representation. If capital were supplied him, if he "had Bill Gates's fortune," he says, he "would build the city of the future," and in this city "what will occupy people won't be work" but "study, art, sport, and festival."[41] Even when short the capital, though, Coppola's career is marked by his endeavors to enact social plans in what we might consider scaled settings. American Zoetrope would deregulate the workplace by enthroning art as its business principle. He started a "new operation," he said at the time, "with the means of making films at intelligent costs," because he had "good relationships with and promises from some of the more talented young filmmakers around."[42] "The conditions under which Francis wanted everyone to work were more than spartan," the filmmaker Carol Ballard once said. "They were practically non-earning."[43] But "being spartan," Coppola thought, "not only greatly reduces overhead but also destroys the hierarchy that affects a company when its people care only about their bonuses."[44] This notion of subtracting profit from business enterprise, we should note, is not strictly Coppola's crackpot thinking, for Peter Drucker, whose influence in management theory is unrivaled, would define it as the essence of business. In *The Practice of Management,* Drucker asserts that "profitability is not the purpose of business enterprise" and the existence of the "so-called 'profit motive' . . . is highly doubtful."[45] Rather, a good business is defined through the capacity its culture of ideas has to "create a customer"; profit can only signal the "validity" of its "business behavior."[46] In Coppola's general disregard for money, we see that he begins to orient business by something more durable still: a set of ideas.

The Cinema of Finance Capital

An important quality to remark in *Tucker* is that in it Coppola means to secure a legacy for Preston Tucker that has very little to do with the car he designed for production. In the movie's final scene, when people file from the courtroom to see the Tucker 48, Abe Karatz says, "Look, they love the car," but seeing their love drives him crazy because "the Tucker Motor Company's dead. They'll never be made." Tucker, in contrast, is satisfied that they made the cars at all; they're a fait accompli for him.

When Abe objects, "Fifty cars," as though the paltry output attests only to their failure to mass produce, Tucker says, "Well, what's the difference, fifty or fifty million—that's only machinery. It's the idea that counts." Indeed, we could say that *Tucker* was more significantly an idea than a movie. It had been the regulating idea for American Zoetrope since a 1975 interview when Coppola promised "to make a film of Tucker's story someday."[47] At the time, he conceived the movie as "a sort of Brechtian musical in which Tucker would be the main story, but it would also involve Edison and Henry Ford and Firestone and Carnegie."[48] When in 1980 Coppola bought Hollywood General as the new facilities for American Zoetrope, he planned to make *One from the Heart* (1982) as a dry run before making *Tucker*. After doing so, he brought Leonard Bernstein and Betty Comden and Adolph Green to his Napa Valley home to develop *Tucker* in its musical form, but the box-office performance of *One from the Heart* forced him to curtail its development. The form in which *Tucker* finally appeared, not as a musical but as a Capra-like tale whose financial backing was owed to the success of Lucasfilm, might obstruct our view of the ideas behind it. In the coming pages I will discuss the movie's formal complexity, and how Coppola factored such view-obstruction into the movie as a main principle of its form. For now, it's more to the point that Coppola's strange equanimity about American Zoetrope—which for practical purposes was doomed as a studio when Warner Bros. rejected its only production, *THX-1138* (1971)—comes off as a foretaste of Abe's dialogue with Tucker, cited above: "The whole idea of [American Zoetrope] caught the imagination of a lot people," Coppola said a year after the company's so-called Black Thursday (i.e. the Warner withdrawal), "but the impracticality of it proved too great."[49]

If American Zoetrope—as *a firm*—never quite succeeded in making movies but might count as a success anyway because it produced *the idea* for novel forms of manufacture, then it seems apt that Coppola's grandest movie project, *Megalopolis*, was never made and has a legacy, to the extent that it does, only as an idea. From all reports, *Megalopolis* was the story of finance capital, which is a process without a product. The whole project of finance capital, after all, is to continue valorizing capital without commodity production. With *Megalopolis,* Coppola would narrate "efforts to build a utopia in New York" in the aftermath of "a financial crisis modeled on the one the city weathered in the mid-

70s."[50] In this moment, New York City was an experiment in finance capital, with its "massive restructuration in which 750,000 manufacturing jobs . . . disappeared, and in which the ratio of manufacturing to office work [was] modified from 2:1 before the war to 1:2 today."[51] This mutation in an economy, Fernand Braudel argues, is an expected phase of capital in its *longue durée* perspective. We ought, therefore, to imagine New York's replacement of manufacturing jobs with office work as an expression of the same process Hollywood was undergoing during the years Coppola was starting his career. Hollywood abandoned fixed production, its celebrated studio system, in part for the external reason that the 1948 Paramount decree cut the circuit between production and circulation, and in part because television signaled an altogether new kind of circulation. We should not, however, overlook the internal reason that the rising cost and systemic inflexibility of fixed production meant a falling rate of profit for Hollywood's mode of production.

For present purposes, then, we must understand finance capital not only as a fully historical moment but as Coppola's moment. When postwar Hollywood was reorganized by independent production, many assessed this independence in honorific terms. But the companies that helped undo Hollywood's vertical integration, however independent, were less a heroic redefinition of the industry than a meliorative response to its stagnancy. "If Hollywood is changing," Coppola had soberly assessed, "then it's because the whole world is changing."[52] This is what his more political-minded contemporaries in the New Left would observe in their famous manifesto, the Port Huron Statement, which remarked how "suddenly the number of workers producing goods became fewer than the number in 'nonproductive' areas—government, trade, finance, services, utilities, transportation. Since World War II 'white collar' and 'service' jobs have grown twice as fast as have 'blue collar' production jobs. Labor has almost no organization in the expanding occupational areas of the new economy."[53] The New Left's organizing statement, that is, called attention to the disorganizing effect that capital had on labor, once Fordism no longer brokered their truce. What some call post-Fordism, others call informal economy, and still others call "disorganized capitalism."[54]

In the face of this, Coppola had meant to keep production intact by making it more lean through technology and information. Throughout his career he would continue to bet on America as the unit of new economy if not always the site, he would later say, because it had "a tremendous tradition of creativity." But its creative labor could only reorganize if those framing it (and the identity of "those" framers, if nebulous, we must imagine to be the usual suspects: state officials, industry captains, corporations) were to seize on such new technologies as "high definition television" "tied to one international standard" such that, for instance, "the concept of world television" could be realized.[55] Technology, for Coppola, tends to deliver labor from whatever its straits, *in potentia,* and the "electronic cinema" was long his pet figure for integral labor. But America would need to adapt its juridical framework—"one international standard," that is—because the pressures of a world system meant that capital would otherwise be valorized abroad. In the movie industry, this is now known as Global Hollywood.[56] Giovanni Arrighi argues that precisely in this change in the "spatial configuration," with production moving "from high-income to low-income countries and regions," do we recognize the onset of finance capital.[57] Coppola, unlike many of his peers, claims our interest because he is at once an agent in this process and the narrator of it. In what follows I'll track the conjugation of Coppola's technological utopianism from the in-transit production of *The Rain People,* a practice otherwise called "runaway production," into its most grandiloquent exposition in *Apocalypse Now* (1979). There, the catastrophic side of the "one international standard" is indexed in the effort of bringing the so-called Third World under it.

Only with *Apocalypse Now,* we might say, did Coppola begin to understand his projects in a political register. He would claim that when he and George Lucas founded American Zoetrope, they were very much "not political."[58] This makes sense, given that in the late 1960s "political" behavior was popularly identified with the protesters Nixon called "noise-makers." But Coppola's emphasis on production, his goal of "having all the means of production readily available" to him, became more legibly political to him only when the stakes of production were cast in geopolitical terms. When, for instance, Coppola was "frustrated" because he needed Philippine air force helicopters for his Vietnam movie on the same day they were needed to fight rebels "in the hills about ten miles away" from their film set, his ambitions—with business and aesthetic ideas folded together—became clear to him in their fuller dimension.[59] His work needed to gauge its effects in a world-historical purview, needed an impossible view that might give measure of all forces as they interact with each other, and this, ultimately, set an internal limit on the future he and Lucas envisioned for American Zoetrope.

Lucas, by contrast, preferred buffering his own work against the socioeconomic forces external to it. Consider, in this respect, his first two movies, *THX-1138* and *American Graffiti* (1973). The former movie is interested in depicting spaces of production. In it, we see a spectacle of clean and technological labor, seemingly a droid assembly (a preview of C-3PO), but the point being made is that the workers are themselves doing droid's work. Nothing more than extensions of the total laboring apparatus, the workers are clad in white scrubs and skull caps; they are drugged into a kind of symbiosis with the machine operations. Indeed, the branches of the operation are satirically named—Department of Biological Flow—so as to underscore how inorganic and artificial this site of labor is. It does not look like the interiors of an American corporation, in short, but is an exaggeration and transformation of whatever is most phenomenologically oppressive in such labor. It transforms such sites, then, into art objects.[60] "If I had put everyone in crew cuts and gray suits," Lucas remarked, then audiences would have understood it as an "abstraction of 1970."[61] But in some sense one assumes that the laboring situation of 1970 is so highly mediated in *THX* because only in raising such rote precision-work into an aesthetic order does it become acceptable for Lucas. The more abstract, the better. At a certain level of abstraction, there is no need to narrate the passage from the site of production to its yield, the product. And indeed, the difficulty Lucas faced when converting it from abstract film into feature film was that its mise-en-scène would not accept the implantation of narrative—not gracefully, anyway. Lucas preferred "documentaries and abstract films," he has always claimed, and would rather have retreated into institutions of the avant-garde as had his Zoetrope colleague, John Korty, who had, with Stan Vanderbeek, "shared billing on the first program in America that used the term 'underground cinema.'" But Coppola would not sequester his work, nor the work of his peers, from society at large; he would shield it with corporate form but would not let it be pigeonholed as coterie activity.

Though the sites of production seem dystopian,
THX-1138 presents them as art objects.

Hence *THX* is a conflicted statement from American Zoetrope, because in the movie's commitment to dystopian outlooks on scientifically managed labor, it cannot imagine its way outside the bifurcation of labor and consumption. Its computers order workers, "Buy more, buy more now, buy and be happy," and in this it's hard to see consumption as anything but another version of labor—bled white of pleasure, it's only another of the boss's commands. The movie views consumption *as* labor, void of pleasure, where Zoetrope viewed labor as a version of consumption, full of pleasure. Infrastructure, in *THX*, can only threaten one. "We could leave," LUH tells THX, "and live in the superstructure." In this submission to a two-world structure—our enslaved labor on one side, and our liberated consumption on the other side—*THX* can only represent the terms American Zoetrope was meant to cancel. THX does finally, in the story's finale, escape the infrastructure, though there is little optimism that he has escaped to a better place.

We might imagine, as a kind of thought experiment, that he has escaped into Lucas's *American Graffiti*, a world of hot rods, pop songs, and all the sumptuary objects that let one forget the deadening labors of one's daytime. That here infrastructure and superstructure remain always asunder, however, might count as an effect of American Zoetrope's failure. In what follows I will describe American Zoetrope as a business idea, Coppola's in better part, that would rely on aesthetic means to manifest itself, and I will tell the story of American Zoetrope, in turn, by way of the vicissitudes an aesthetic project like this must travel. The effort to merge business activity and aesthetic experience seems, after all, typical of the 1960s. If originally the project seemed politically innocent, it's likely because such matters of art, the workplace, and consumption had been viewed—by Coppola, Lucas, and others—from the perspective of San Francisco. If *THX* renders infrastructure (the Gas and Electric Building, the BART system, and so on) not a practical matter but an aesthetic one, we can guess that it squares with the felt needs of an educated class in general, no matter how "underground" such needs were declared. But when for the sake of a movie Coppola brought his own generator to Baler, a Filipino town without electricity since it had been "destroyed in a typhoon" ten years earlier and was "never replaced," something of the "contradictory forces at work in such a production," as Miriam Hansen puts it, would give a political character to Coppola's work.[62] Henceforth there would be a more complex sense of social totality—a sense, I argue, that Coppola had courted—in which Zoetrope's business and aesthetic ideas would try to find their place.

At best, these ideas found their place intermittently—often compromised, sometimes fully defeated. This book means to be a record of the forms allowed these ideas. In this endeavor, my study looks at Coppola from a slightly unfamiliar perspective. The most rehearsed critical perspective on Coppola is that he was a Hollywood outsider, too much a dreamer to be a foursquare businessman, and that it was his creative temperament that left him outside—even safeguarded him against—the domains of commerce. This outlook depends on two academic prejudices: first, that business is not creative, despite all signs otherwise, and second, that any art that makes money becomes harder to recognize as art. My position on Coppola, rather, is that he innovated precisely *from within* Hollywood's industrial system; that he took business and art to be coequal terms, each depending on the other for its wholeness (he had a grudge against Hollywood not because it was business when it should be art, but because as a business it was poorly run, with too little art and pleasure in its practices); and that he appreciated corporate form, particularly the vexed idea of corporate personhood, to the extent that it was aesthetically construed.

Coppola's notion of the aesthetic dimension of the corporation, I argue, was that it required a figure of unity only possessed by opera.

Critics regularly deem Coppola operatic, but when the concept is rigorously applied rather than remarked in passing, critics tend to see opera only as what haunts his films, and sometimes even what gives them deep structure. I make the strong claim, instead, that operatic structure gives shape to his film and business projects alike. Opera, many have argued, is a display of voice subtended by transpersonal forces, wherein what looks like the autonomization of the voice—the aria—is given its place, ecstatic as it seems, by the community of voices. It is structurally unlike lyric voice, a singular, individual voice that is part of the song tradition drawn upon and sublated in opera. Family works on opera's model, in Coppola's philosophy, as does a corporation. The corporation makes sense, in his view, to the extent that the integrity of its enterprise is vouchsafed in a transferrable voice—that is, a non-dominating or *operatic* voice. His movies can be analyzed as efforts to give what are often reified themes (family, corporate personhood) the vitality of aesthetic form (opera). Insofar as Coppola's ideas successfully took root, and even insofar as they were perverted, his innovations belong to business history as much as aesthetic history. In the coming pages, I establish that the consistently unsettling problem of how to mark groups as undivided entities—a problem of modernity insofar as traditional society never required rational proof for it—has found varied solutions in the history of political form (the nation-state), business form (the corporation), and aesthetic form (the opera). These histories cross-pollinate throughout intellectual history, and Coppola is an illuminating nodal point in such a study.

In what follows, I will assess a set of Coppola's movies in relation to what I'm calling his business idea (that production be animated by the same pleasures as consumption, that production and consumption happen in view of each other) and to what I'm calling his aesthetic take on the business firm. Because I assess Coppola's career in this way, brushing somewhat against the grain of critical orthodoxies, I put pressure on some works long considered minor, such as *Tucker,* and I ignore some works altogether, such as *The Outsiders* (1982), *The Cotton Club* (1984), and *Bram Stoker's Dracula* (1992). This should not be taken as a silent verdict on the merit of those movies. My discussion isn't guided by merit alone but rather by how much Coppola's business idea penetrates the content and form of his movies. This being so, I start by analyzing *The*

Rain People (1969) as the manifesto of American Zoetrope, one more attuned to the upstart firm's corporate purpose than its first movie, *THX-1138*, would end up being. While not operatic in the least, *The Rain People* is a poetic film, one that might count as a poetics of political economy. It is of aesthetic interest because it eschews the pop-song soundtrack and Hollywood-musical form of Coppola's previous films, *You're a Big Boy Now* and *Finian's Rainbow*; it is of business interest because its making doubled as the making of American Zoetrope.

From here, I consider a series of Coppola's movies that were deeply informed by Zoetrope's failure—*The Godfather, The Conversation* (1974), and *Tucker*—each of which I take to be a meditation on, and in moments an argument for, corporate purpose. This account of Coppola's business ideas flows into an inquiry into his aesthetic ideas, starting with opera as a bedeviled form of modernism in *Apocalypse Now,* and then as a form tested anew and reconsidered in *The Godfather, Part III* (1990) and *Tetro* (2009), and, finally, ending with forms of musical decomposition (i.e. the song collection, the jukebox, the album)—or what becomes Zoetrope 2.0 when Sofia and Roman Coppola inherit their father's firm, what I'll also call "Zoetrope postmodernism"—in *One from the Heart* and later in Sofia's movies, namely *The Virgin Suicides* (1999) and *Marie Antoinette* (2006).

Hippies, Inc: *The Rain People*
and the Making of American Zoetrope

When in 1969 the Las Vegas tycoon Kirk Kerkorian bought a controlling share in MGM only to gut the firm by liquidating "$62 million in company assets over the next four years, including its Culver City backlots, its Boreham Wood studio in London (MGM British), MGM Records, and fifty years of costumes and props," he became only the most outrageous agent of Hollywood's transition into finance capital.[63] Many of the studios bought and absorbed into conglomerates in this era had been valued as brands, as real estate to be parceled and sold, and, in the main, as liquid assets. What was most "outrageous" about Kerkorian is that, unlike the Gulf and Western CEO Charles Bluhdorn, he didn't even seem to care about movies; he was simply a corporate raider to whom the bearishly trading Hollywood studios looked like dollars. In using the brand for his MGM Grand Hotel, he showed interest in corporate identity but not much concern for how it derived.

In this historical moment, Francis Ford Coppola and George Lucas were trying to pass from being the standout students at their respective film schools to being figures of consequence in Hollywood industry. Coppola had been well known at UCLA for having made inroads into the industry. He had won the Samuel Goldwyn Award for his original screenplay, *Pilma Pilma,* a prize that can earmark talent for industry admission.[64] He had also begun working for Roger Corman, the "engineer," as Coppola called him, of exploitation cinema.[65] Corman, in fact, took out space in the trade papers to announce Coppola's Samuel Goldwyn Award.[66] Fellow students viewed Coppola, he himself claims, as "the original sellout."[67] In the meantime, George Lucas was the student across town developing a reputation as the "legend" of USC. Not as enterprising as Coppola, Lucas nonetheless impressed his cohort, including Walter Murch and Caleb Deschanel, with short films such as "The Emperor" and "THX-1138 4EB."

Though Coppola was more boldly business-minded, he and Lucas shared a critique of big institutions—an antiestablishment view, if you like—that made reimagining business practices a first step on their career path. This critique did not make them loners but rather members of the burgeoning counterculture, which in the Port Huron Statement designated its opponents as Big Government, Big Military, Big Business, and Big Labor too. If the document's authors, the Students for a Democratic Society (SDS), would be remembered for addressing their most concerted efforts to government reform, it should not now be forgotten how centrally workplace reform figured in their statement. Organized labor, in their view, had "succumbed to institutionalization, its social idealism waning under the tendencies of bureaucracy, materialism, business ethics."[68] If SDS did not make its mark in business reform, Coppola and Lucas would. Their disdain of workplaces in which "the individual is regulated as part of the system," and their unwillingness to "tolerate meaningless work"—to crib words from the Port Huron Statement—meant that their countercultural appearances would do the job of declaring them outsiders of the very industry they were busy making their way inside.[69] When Coppola met Lucas on a Warner Bros. backlot, they gravitated to each other because they were "both very young" and "both had beards."[70]

Coppola was on the Warner lot because he was, in perhaps a misconceived choice on his part and the studio's, directing the Fred Astaire vehicle *Finian's Rainbow*. On making *You're a Big Boy Now*, an opportunity granted him by way of his screenwriting services for Seven Arts, Coppola seemed the right (in his telling, a cheap) director for *Finian* after the Warner–Seven Arts merger. Giving him a dated musical, the studio hoped that Coppola could "zip it up and do it à la *Big Boy*," which is to say they thought he might infuse "youthfulness" in a pat formula. He did update it in some respects, such as casting the African American botanist, Howard, to resemble Stokely Charmichael. This, however, is where the seams most showed, the problem being, in Coppola's eyes, "how to reconcile the traditions of a 1940s musical theater" with civil rights and other issues of the "contemporary time."[71]

The musical was by then an old and favorite genre of Jack Warner's that had been exhausted, as the recent box office of *Camelot* (1967) suggested. The whole operation looked shabby enough that when Coppola found Lucas on set and asked what he was looking at, Lucas replied, "Nothing much." Lucas was there after winning a six-month Warner Bros. scholarship over fellow finalist Walter Murch, with whom he, while awaiting the scholarship decision, entered a pact to work cooperatively in future projects. Lucas came to the studio, history would have it, to observe its moribund culture. He hoped to learn from the animation department, but it had been shuttered at roughly the time he arrived. By default, Lucas was left to observe *Finian's Rainbow*, the only movie then in production on the lot.

What Coppola and Lucas were witnessing, and in some sense intuitively comprehending, was the decay of one style of studio management. Not only because the movie in production was the last made under the "aegis" of the firm's namesake, Jack Warner, as Ronald Colby claims. Not only because they were "the only two people on the set who were under 50."[72] And not only because it made no sense to apply the kinetic pacing of Coppola's *Big Boy*, modeled as it was on Richard Lester's Beatles movies, to a latter-day Fred Astaire musical. But, more basically, because the Warner management layer was unsettled by changing ownership. Soon it would stabilize, when Warner Bros. was purchased by the conglomerate Kinney National Services Inc., and a new class of managers was installed. Until then, Coppola and Lucas critically beheld

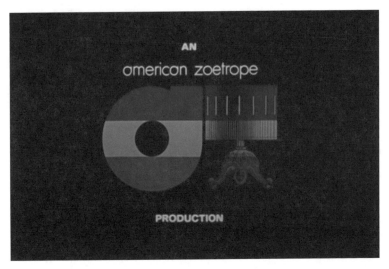

The American Zoetrope corporate logo. |

the "vacuum" that needed filling. In their discontent was the germ of American Zoetrope.

In order to construct their own studio, though, they would need to make a movie. The firm American Zoetrope, in a curious way, is first explicated by the movie they made, *The Rain People*. This might not seem so curious. Given that their craft was moviemaking, how better to assert their professional prerogative than through plying their craft conspicuously well? What seems curious about Coppola, though, is how deeply he seemed to hold the conviction that prior to making a movie— or any product, for that matter—one must first make a satisfying site for one's labor. Hollywood, as he found it, was "a sad, pent-up place."[73] By his lights, it ought to "be providing not only a product, something it can sell, but a hospitable place for creative people to work."[74] The identity between a product and the site of its making is so complete for Coppola, with the structure of the one mirroring the other, that the imaginary dimension of his movie, *The Rain People*, became a key resource for envisioning the ethical life of the firm, American Zoetrope. That art often imagines a better world is commonplace enough; that movies should imagine a better movie studio, less so.

The Rain People, a Coppola-Lucas collaboration of sorts, was a countercultural statement on screen and off, bent toward imagining studio operations in terms congenial to youth culture. What was put *on* screen largely owes to Coppola, as the plot had splintered from his student screenplay, *The Gray Stationwagon,* which followed three women who had left their husbands.[75] The three separate story arcs seemed "too ambitious" for their modest budget—$750,000 from Kenny Hyman at Warner–Seven Arts—and would have involved a social dimension, cutting against the lyric states that are the movie's core element. From the larger story Coppola culled the story of Natalie Ravenna, a recently married woman who awakes one morning determined to leave her husband, we infer, because she married too young, is now pregnant, and feels stultified by her suburban life. She drives cross-country, early on picking up a mentally disabled hitchhiker, Jimmy Kilgannon, whom she cannot shake thereafter. True to the picaresque tale, no plot takes hold—only a series of disconnected adventures. Some critics have called it a "road movie in the classic sense."[76]

This "classic" designation, however, overlooks the significance of it being a woman who has left home not in search of herself, as is typically the case for male protagonists in the American romance, but in flight from her circumscribed role in the family. The movie trades on Betty Friedan's "problem that has no name."[77] In *The Feminine Mystique,* Friedan says, "Sometimes a woman would tell me that the feeling gets so strong she runs out of the house and walks through the street."[78] She notes, too, an article run by *McCall's* in 1956 called "The Mother Who Ran Away" that "brought the highest readership of any article they had ever run."[79] These are more fugitive stories than they are quest narratives. If on the surface we see the story of a woman's boredom, her isolated moods and subjective dispositions as she goes to encounter a new range of experience—the surface Coppola commits to film—in another register we see the rejection of one regime of labor, deeply entrenched in postwar culture. The protagonist is a woman because, in this regime, it falls to women to reproduce the values of such labor in their children; and she is a woman because Fordism has confined her "to the domestic routine of the housewife," in Friedan's phrase, in an inverted image of her husband's public routine of the company man.[80] The two spheres, necessary complements that they are, must be critiqued at once. This, we might say, is the reason the historian Daniel Horowitz argues that we must understand Friedan's work as a labor journalist in the 1950s before we understand her feminist manifesto of the 1960s. The "mechanized housework," so Horowitz says, was one expression of the economy that mechanized labor *tout court*.[81]

The gesture that Coppola and Lucas made *off* screen, I contend, is meant to reflect and put itself in a mutually clarifying relationship with Natalie's gesture on screen. First they fled Hollywood to make the movie, opting to shoot it anywhere but there: at Hofstra, on location in Pennsylvania, West Virginia, Tennessee, and Kentucky, before establishing a beachhead in "an abandoned shoe shop" in Ogallala, Nebraska.[82] The film crew occupied the store and shipped in extra editing gear so they could begin "a full-scale editing" of the movie-in-progress away from the supervision of Warner–Seven Arts, in a move that would become characteristic for Coppola, who, even when making the *Godfather* movies squarely within Hollywood, would find clauses to let him do post-production work elsewhere, in both cases San Francisco. The press called this gesture to carry out their moviemaking in "changing areas of production supervision" a "daring experiment in new production techniques."[83]

Coppola and the small crew traveled in a motorcade of station wagons and microbuses; the most innovative vehicle—dubbed "Silverfish," though the editor Barry Malkin taped a sign on it reading, "The Magical Mystery Tour"—was a fully rigged production facility on wheels (with mixing boards installed within). "Radio communication between the vans was essential," Peter Cowie writes, "as usually the next night's destination was not fixed."[84] Their nomadism let them slip Hollywood unions, but it added the diplomatic task of getting shooting permission in the random municipalities. Hence, once they left New York, Lucas relates, "[E]verybody had to get a haircut and shave their beards off" so that, as incognito hippies, they could "get the cooperation of the various cities and towns that [they'd] go through in order to be able to shoot."[85]

In part this caravan lifestyle placed them at a remove—"We were isolated and on our own," Robert Duvall recalls—so that they would be allowed to create a business culture of their own that they could then transplant to San Francisco, the final destination not for the movie alone but for American Zoetrope, the firm being germinated by the movie. That was the final term, after all, and the movie was but a means for it. Making *The Rain People,* by every account, was fun for all involved. "Those of us who went along," Coppola notes, "including Jimmy Caan and Bobby Duvall, still talk about the cookouts in the back of the sound trailer."[86] The pleasure, though, was professional pleasure. The cinematographer, Bill Butler, impressive as his credits are (*Jaws* [1975], *One Flew over the Cuckoo's Nest* [1975], *Grease* [1978]), still counts *The Rain People* as one of his best jobs. The challenge of having only a "minimum number of lights" was considerable, he recalls, but Coppola "gives you a lot of freedom. He lets your creativity work for him."[87] Like Preston Tucker, one might say. Coppola would call this his "creative management."[88] It forced one to be inventive, Butler says, and Coppola "loves that particular kind of inventiveness anyway." Butler continues, "I don't believe I've pulled off more special things for anyone than I have for him."[89]

Let's consider *The Rain People* as an experiment in new relations: labor relations on the set, family relations in the film narrative, and all these, combined, making for social relations. We should dwell for a moment on the movie itself, in its capacity as social text. In an effort to forge new relations, the movie sets itself the task of imagining old ones, as they disintegrate, becoming the chrysalis for new ones. Unlike Coppola's subsequent movies, such as *The Conversation, Tucker,* or the *Godfather* movies in their criminal way, *The Rain People* does not

Sociality on the set of *The Rain People.* |

depict the site of labor. It depicts, rather, the economic substructure that is the ground for labor. The movie begins with a peremptory refusal of old relations, and the labor regime they fortify, when Natalie (Shirley Knight) decides to leave her husband. Its most daring move is the suppression of any direct cause for her decision, situating the story this way shoulder-to-shoulder with the existential cinema of Europe, in particular Michelangelo Antonioni's *L'Avventura* (1960). Coppola says, in fact, that he screened a rough cut of his movie for Antonioni, who "liked it very much."[90]

Natalie, in this act, refuses family as given. This alone led many to claim *The Rain People* as an early feminist movie, and further justification for the claim is that the movie created a complex role for Shirley Knight in an era when women had few such roles available to them. Knight seemed, Coppola says, "like an American actress who had some substance."[91] A more thoroughgoing logic for the claim is that feminism understands, and brings to light, the social construction of the putative naturalness of family relations. In the first sequence of the movie, Natalie does precisely this. She flees her husband in the early-morning hours and visits her mother, from whom, it seems, she expects sympathy. She gets only her mother's bafflement, which marks the generational difference between the women. But when her father enters the room, the scene is instantly reordered. The two women had been held in a single frame. But the father's entrance, his mere presence, is felt—before it registers visually or aurally—in a cut to Natalie, isolated in a profile shot, who is then "hailed" by the voice of the Father. "Hi, Nat," he says, in loving fatherly tones. It is the abruptness of the edit, though, and the faintly religious character of Natalie's posture—the meek surrender of a supplicant—that give the scene the rhythms of authority unquestioned and unopposed. "Is it alright if I talk in my own house?" he will shortly bark at his wife. No more loving tones, once pressed.

The Rain People gathers its force as social critique, such that it is, through formal nuance. While Coppola would go on to master a kind of social narrative, the *Godfather* movies being the finest example, this movie is more like a poem. "It achieves," Peter Cowie remarks, "a blank verse quality of its own."[92] Its poetics are deployed to operate at the level of subjectivity, its making and unmaking, its finally liquid condition being marked in the movie's title. I will address only a few, representative nuances in its form. Two aspects, Coppola's precise dialogue and Shirley Knight's flat affect, work in combination. In the dialogue we find a play on pronouns—for instance, the possessory edge the father so easily gives the phrase "my own house." On hearing it, the audience knows implicitly how naturally he inhabits his role in the family structure, how needless a quibble he would find it to say *our* house rather than *my* house.

The concern with pronominal identification (I am I, you are you) is elaborated in a subsequent scene. In flight from home, Natalie stops at a gas station along the Pennsylvania Turnpike and calls her husband, Vinny. He tells her to come home, but she declines. "I just had to get away for a while," Natalie explains. "The married lady, she was getting desperate." She begins shifting between first- and third-person pronouns, displacing in her handling of grammar her own experience from the structure meant to contain it. This is, on the one hand, a question of who can possess: before marriage, Natalie says, "I would wake up in the morning and it was my day, and now it belongs to you." Vinny can possess, while she cannot, not by decree of patriarchal arrangements. On the other hand, what is at stake is Natalie's capacity to identify with the roles on offer. This can come off as madness: "She's pregnant," Natalie confesses to Vinny. "She, me, your wife." It is better understood, however, as a keen sensitivity to the self-alienation so essential to Fordism; the condition under which one labors, in this system, is in a highly specialized role within a total operation, but in such a way that

Natalie Ravenna understands herself from subjective and objective standpoints at once, making her seem a split personality.

one is individually alienated from the yield of that labor. Natalie's aware-ness looks neurotic, even crazy, because she is divorced (to pun on the marriage contract) from her role and is attuned instead to the system enfolding it. Her experience is no longer ground-level but is rather that of the administrator-on-high. Her marriage, experienced objectively rather than subjectively, lacks the additive that makes the institution seem emotional rather than what it is, legal.

She takes care to tell Vinny, "It's not you, it's not you, it isn't," and while this rings with a familiar breakup rhetoric, we can understand it—having tracked the pronoun tensions—to be an entirely true statement. Not only is her husband, Vinny, guilty of nothing in particular; he is absent in any substantial form from the narrative. We hear his voice in a phone receiver, like a sound from the past that travels more slowly to us than the visual sign of a phenomenon. Mathias Nilges has argued that a narrative pattern of lost fathers is a symptom of the transition out of Fordism. If Henry Ford himself counted as the archetypal strong father—as seen, for instance, in Upton Sinclair's fictional account, *The Flivver King,* where Abner Shutt takes not only a salary from Ford but also advice from the latter's *Dear-born Independent*—it is because he ordered the world of work through centralized authority. With Fordism outmoded, now a subject "roaming the world, an orphaned, involuntary nomad in search of [a] lost father" marks "a large-scale transformation in the socioeconomic structure that leaves behind Fordism's paternalistic logic."[93]

It is during the confrontation between mother and father, when the father asks if he can talk in his "own house," that the movie formally undoes its investment in the family as structuring principle. First we see the parents in contention, but then we flash back to the scene of Natalie's wedding, with people dancing joyously in a ring. Their joy, however, assumes a malevolent quality when juxtaposed against the quarreling parents, with the father's domination taken so thoroughly for granted. If Natalie's wedding memories once had the effect of binding her to family, these memories have now been emptied of their affective content. Natalie's flat affect throughout the movie, then, comes from her lost object of cathexis. Its patriarch now demystified, the society to come is of indeterminate character.

Natalie herself might will it into being, if she can flee the grips of the old world. What she does, however, is reconstruct the dead patriarch, this time in the form of a football player, Jimmy "Killer" Kilgannon (James Caan), once a stock figure of masculinity but here a cipher. Killer suffered a head injury at Belmont College, we discover, and having been paid hush money to leave school, he is now, for all purposes, an orphan on the road. There is something perverse in his figure, as though the movie has begun to roll back Natalie's father's masculine authority and show it in regressive stages. In Killer, Natalie has a man-child that, in moments, she enjoys manipulating. She plays him a game of Simon Says, for instance. Her pleasure ends, though, when she sees the long scar on his head. It seems that the sight of this diminished football player—the effigy of bygone authority—saps Natalie of whatever residual affections she had for the family structure. She is sickened by Killer now, and is receding farther from her husband, too.

From here, the movie becomes more and more awkwardly emplotted. The figure of natural authority, Killer, is swapped out for a figure of formal authority, Officer Gordon (Robert Duvall). Neither is credible authority. It all concludes with Killer, the sacrificial innocent, dying in Natalie's arms. Had the movie been a short subject, limited to the opening stanza of her flight and her defense of it to her husband, it would be a well-wrought poem. In the form of a narrative, though, the movie's stabs at mapping the social world (when what it seemed good at was capturing the lyrical disorder of the subject) dissipate its overall impact. From reports, we know that the shooting script was incomplete when the road trip began.[94] It was worked out impromptu with the actors, often in the morning before shooting, or the story took shape simply from events in progress, town by town. It had all emerged, anyway, from an image—"the idea of a woman just leaving and staying in a motel," Coppola says—and whatever might flow from this image would, as a matter of course, constitute the movie.[95] "Improvisation was the keynote," Peter Cowie says. "In Chattanooga, Tennessee, Coppola learned that an Armed Forces Day parade was about to take place, so decided to use it as background."[96]

If few people today group *The Rain People* with Coppola's great movies, or even recall it at all, it might stem from the movie having planted its feet in the different, perhaps immiscible spheres of private and public experience. An image of subjective inwardness, that is, became the object of group collaboration. The film crew, prompted by Coppola, was telling the story of subjectivity, each day at work, but the subjectivity they were asked to narrate was the kind that could hold in place as the first term of a new economy. Coppola's later movies often behold the economy from a topological standpoint. This movie is committed, by contrast, to working out what we might call a tropological standpoint on the economy—a set of tropes that from their narrow vantage could give figure to a much larger field of activity. How, the movie asks, does the image of the fugitive housewife alone in a motel give rise to the image of a different social world?

I'm tempted to say this is more than the film medium would bear for Coppola, at least at this point in his career. The movie's title, in any case, calls attention to its system of tropes. A certain amount of poetic data was forgiven the film image—was withheld, too, from its narration—and was commuted instead to language. The "rain people," as Killer describes them in conversation with Natalie, are "people made of rain, and when they cry they disappear altogether because they cry themselves away." Peter Cowie, echoing several critics, finds the line pretentious.[97] But when Killer explains that "they look like ordinary people, only she is very, very beautiful and he is handsome," we sense that the movie can only render its main theme in Killer's limited perspective: the ideals that make a social structure durable—Hollywood's beautiful dream, say, of the man and woman at the center of the nuclear family—can only be seen for their evanescence by the village fool, Killer, precisely because he, unlike Natalie, has had all his social programming cleared by compulsion (brain trauma) rather than by volition (self-knowledge).

If an artless device, it nonetheless explains why rain is the element of the movie. Consider, for instance, the opening shot of a neighborhood street taken from a worm's-eye view. In it, a garbage truck moves toward us, but what we see most prominently, as a function of our extreme low angle, is puddled water with rain dappling its surface. Over that patch of screen appears the movie title. The following shots are largely of water; the effects of rain, mostly, but we also see Natalie in the shower. The opening sequence of the movie deploys water imagery for some effect, and the title affirms the thematic centrality of the effect. Water is the element of the movie, we will see, because it contrasts with solid-state stability. It contrasts with concrete structure, with reified social roles, with Killer the football player, Gordon the police officer, and Natalie the housewife.

A concept from Gilles Deleuze might let us clarify how this trope gives, or might hope to give, traction on a larger field of relations. In theorizing cinema, Deleuze names a certain phase or orientation of the perception-image, "liquid perception."[98] Within a large phylum he calls the movement-image (the *"movement-image* and *flowing-matter* are strictly the same thing," Deleuze says, "a world of universal variation, of universal undulation, universal rippling"), Deleuze locates the perception-image, which is a gap between "the action and the reaction."[99] When something is acted on, and there occurs an interval before its reaction to the stimulus, we have proof of "living images"; the other "images," as he calls them, "act and react on all their facets and in all their parts."[100] Quoting Henri Bergson, Deleuze explains that living beings "allow to pass through them, so to speak, those external influences which are indifferent to them; the others isolated, become 'perceptions' by their very isolation."[101] Deleuze understands this operation as precisely a *"framing,"* and he thereby takes the cinema as a figure for understanding perception as it rises and falls, is made and unmade, on the larger plane of matter. It was the French school, Deleuze claims, that discovered a subjective frame (i.e. perception), but their habit, as Jean Renoir's "predilection for running water" evinces, was to place this frame in motion, such that the subject never enjoys a stable hold on itself.[102] The medium of water, for them, suggested the making and unmaking of perception, and hence the possible dissolution of the subject. Deleuze calls this "liquid perception" and says that it requires us to imagine "a race of men" that breaks "links" with solid earth, "father with son, husband with wife and mistress, woman with lover, children with parents."[103] The limit case of such cinema would be "a drama without characters."[104] Perhaps Joris Ivens's *Rain* (1929) is the ur-text for this "liquid abstract."[105] In any case, we might begin to interpret Natalie's radical break with family, with foundations as such, by way of the water imagery of the opening sequence. The worm's-eye view that initiates the movie can be taken as the standpoint of the water, pooling on the street, and if we think of "an eye in matter," in a Deleuzian experiment, we would have to imagine that the water thinks of the asphalt as being impermanent, porous, and not at all solid.[106] What from afar seems a solid mass would seem, from the standpoint of particle-life, to be matter easily seeped into and eroded.

While Deleuze often speaks in the language of cosmology ("a state of matter too hot to be able to distinguish solid bodies"), I suggest that we take him here as a thinker of political economy, dedicated, in particular, to cracking the difficulty intrinsic in conceptualizing the open dynamics of an economy.[107] His concepts, after all, are often crypto-Marxist, as readers of his and Félix Guattari's two-volume *Capitalism and Schizophrenia* will recall from its brilliant acts of transcoding. When Deleuze describes the "Open," which refers to the ceaseless reframing of perspective—by turn, the integration of a single-point perspective into the sets of all activity beyond the frame—I suggest that we take this as an able concept for an economy's dynamic operation,[108] and for capitalist economy, to wit, which gains vigor through its capacity to subsume all practices once alien to it. "A closed system is never absolutely closed," Deleuze says. "On the one hand, it is connected in space to other systems by a more or less 'fine' thread, and on the other hand it is integrated or reintegrated into a whole which transmits a duration to it along this thread."[109] Deleuze's description can double as an account of capitalism's inclusionary power in a fashion akin to Joseph Schumpeter's efforts to understand the economy *in time.*

Why we should take our thinking in this direction is justified by the imaginative hold this model of economic thought would come to exercise in American culture from the postwar moment to the turn of the millennium. Schumpeter, matched with the Mont Pelerin economists, helped eventually to displace equilibrium models to one side, and Keynesian models predicated on a closed nation to the other side. Brought to bear on *The Rain People,* a modest perspective indeed on this unfolding history, what we see is not some cosmological perspective on rain. In the opening sequence, rather, we see a highly restricted locus: the suburb, the emblem of postwar economic stability and of orderly family life. The rain, most basically, signals the fluidity of this arrangement. Natalie's neighborhood will in time be awash in finance capital, as the ownership society ushered in by postwar mortgage programs rested on a version of wealth that does not entail production, only underlying assets. From our moment in history, we can easily enough narrate Natalie's moment this way: her role in the home would dissolve in the element of finance capital. Water, we learned the hard way, is a watchword in finance capital. In Natalie's moment—which is to say in Betty Friedan's moment, too—one's eye was likely trained on the task at hand rather than, say, the media conglomerates that were busy liquidating studio holdings to cash out the underlying assets. To think of capital this way, we must first think it through the subjectivities ("angel of the hearth," "domestic goddess," the "happy housewife heroine") it liquidates as it rearranges itself. Natalie is something of a case study in such shape-shifting: her pronoun aphasia is one effect, and the logical corollary to this, her blank affect (she has no self to order affections), is another.

It is a movie that must be understood within two frames. Its story *qua* social text concerns an individual's livelihood. But the production enveloping it—supporting it, we might say—places industrial practices in a frame. For Coppola, these frames had to be seen in view of each other. There had to be a movie, an aesthetic act, as it were, to lay out a business ethos. Ethical commitments first begin in acts of aesthetic reordering. For American Zoetrope, the aesthetic act was *The Rain People*; its ethical counterpart was Lucas's making-of documentary, *Filmmaker*. Coppola had allocated money in the budget for Lucas to shoot a documentary of the movie's production. In tandem, Coppola and Lucas created a movie as American Zoetrope's commodity and also a production mode as its unlikely twin commodity.

The Lucas documentary chronicles an ad hoc manner, rather than a tightly regulated one, in which production might take shape. It was runaway production, first off, which was itself a mode: escaping Los Angeles meant escaping its labor regulations. "Coppola's statements on unions, equipment and management thinking," Dan Simons writes, had been the first phase of his assault on Hollywood practices.[110] In the documentary, he is shown arguing by phone with the director's guild over their insistence that he take a card-carrying assistant director on his project, when he had already opted to use his friend, Bart Patton. This meant, in effect, that he had a redundant position in what was designed as a lean crew. The same sort of battle would play out in San Francisco months later, this time in the trades, when Coppola negoti-ated a concession from the city's craft unions that granted him "full say over daily work patterns so long as he guarantee[d] a 55-hour work week."[111] This flexibility, more than "Hollywood workers ever conceded," signaled that "the union [was] taking cognizance of the special problems of small filmmakers."[112] Making San Francisco "Hollywood North," as some called it, happened because the unions there, as Coppola put it, "are more enthusiastic and cooperative"—that is, they wanted jobs that would otherwise flow to Los Angeles.[113] Coppola would accentuate his small stature as a filmmaker, playing unions off each other, to make a bogey of the big institutions ranged against him.

In *Filmmaker*, Coppola gives a bravura performance. In his telephone argument, it is clear that he means it to be a public display, on camera and likely before the movie crew. Lucas films a performance pitched to his and Coppola's generation of filmmakers. Once *The Rain People* was in the can, Coppola would think of its success as a bellwether for young filmmakers writ large. "The people who will be hurt most" if the movie fails, Coppola says, "will be all those others who feel that a meaningful picture can be brought in on a reasonable budget, and are willing to try something new."[114] On behalf of these filmmakers, therefore, he objects to the director's guild: "Today, you just don't need as many guys." These young filmmakers can make small, non-union movies, Coppola assures the guild. "A lot of my friends who are ready to make films [. . .] are watching very carefully"—hence Coppola's current performance!—"to see if their films can be made within the establishment." If not, and if these young filmmakers defect from unions, Coppla asks, "What do you do if suddenly fifteen of the best America filmmakers don't want any part of the DGA?" The assistant director the DGA assigned him, Coppola later tells the camera, "didn't know what we were doing because he was trained in another kind of filmmaking." In his impromptu style, Coppola was training this upcoming generation in new industrial methods.

What qualified Coppola to lead his filmmaking generation this way, past his having already directed three feature-length movies (one for Corman, *Dementia 13*, and two for Hollywood, *You're a Big Boy Now* and *Finian's Rainbow*), and past his screenwriting credits (numerous by then, but most notably *Patton* [1970]), was his intuition about technology. He believed, and continues to believe, that technology creates a permanent revolution for cinema. When Coppola made ongoing pleas for reasonable budgets, and when he explained that he made *Finian's Rainbow* as a "Roger Corman cheapie" except with "a hell of a lot of guys hanging around," he was rooting his claims in a belief that new technology had outmoded old production routines.[115] After producing *THX-1138*, he would boast, "There's no question that *THX* would have taken 14 weeks for a major Hollywood studio to shoot. We shot it in seven. There's no question that it would have cost them at least $1.5 million; it cost us somewhere near $800,000."[116] But before he could cast off Hollywood's "old-fashioned production equipment," and indeed before he could complete post-production on *The Rain People*, Coppola would need equipment.[117] Once the principal photography was done on *The Rain People*, therefore, he went to the Photokina in Cologne, Germany, where he learned about the leading edge of technology and "became sort of a minor expert" on it, he says, in virtue of inquiring about it. "Much of the problem in American film technology is that everyone's too fast to say, 'It's no good,'" he contended, "but at least I inquired."[118] He returned to the States with a haul that included Steenbeck editing tables and Keller sound mixers. He already owned two 35mm Eclairs, several 16mm Arriflexes, and a "Super-8mm rigged up with a sync-pulse generator."[119] Indeed, in making *The Rain People*, he "rented [his equipment] to the studio, charging it against the budget of the picture."[120]

He needed a facility to house his equipment, however, and hence American Zoetrope was born. It might be worth insisting, rather, that American Zoetrope was born in the acquisition of the technology, not in the leasing of the space. The space did not matter, would not define them, because their utopian spirit rested on the portable technologies that would emancipate the Zoetrope workers from any notion of fixed labor. That was the credo, in that moment. "It was all part of what we saw then," Walter Murch later remarked, "as the beginnings of the technical democratization of the filmmaking process—with comparatively little money you could actually go on the road and shoot a feature film, you could locate wherever you wanted."[121] It is in this respect that American Zoetrope would realize the business reforms the Port Huron Statement called for when it wondered why, "when our own technology is destroying old and creating new forms of social organization," people continued to perform "meaningless work." "This is the time," Coppola would say of Zoetrope, "for this kind of organization."[122]

Coppola's idea for the firm's facility came from his visit, during his trip to Europe, to Mogens Skot-Hansen's Danish studio, Lanterna, which was in fact a mansion located in the countryside. Looking like a European commune, with "pretty Scandinavian girls," as Coppola has commented, it surely evoked the stateside counterculture and the open lifestyle of Vilgot Sjöman's recent sensation, *I Am Curious Yellow* (1967). Without much capital, Coppola and Lucas searched in vain for something comparable outside San Francisco, the city they had chosen as a still-proximate escape from Hollywood. They found, instead, an affordable warehouse space south of Market Street at 827 Folsom Street and began to decorate it after a sixties mod fashion, with a pool table with "a pastel felt top," an espresso machine, and the namesake memento given to Coppola by Skot-Hansen, a Zoetrope. The capital they did have was advanced to them by the new management at Warner Bros., John Calley and Ted Ashley, as part of a seven-picture "first refusal" contract Coppola had negotiated. Some would say, Lucas for instance, that Coppola had buffaloed the executives, who were fresh on the job after Kinney's takeover of the studio. Coppola, the story goes, lied to them that he had a prior agreement with Warner. With the capital outlay, and with the facilities of a nouveau studio, American Zoetrope incorporated on November 12, 1969. Though a corporation in name, they presented themselves in different terms. Hollywood "took a very funny view of the whole enterprise," Coppola says. "They saw this as just an old warehouse with a lot of hippies running around."[123] Indeed, the carpenters building the place, Ronald Colby and others recall, were high on acid while at work. At the studio opening on December 14, 1969, sponsored by Mayor Joseph Alioto's committee on city filmmaking, the celebrities of San Francisco counterculture—Ken Kesey, Bill Graham, Jerry Garcia—were in attendance.

Although the firm was raised on something of a counterculture sensibility, several parts European and several parts stateside, this sensibility was nonetheless compatible with the family structure. Francis's wife, Eleanor Coppola, for instance, designed his office in Swedish modern, "Eames chairs on a gold colored rug." In recalling the corporate digs, she remembers not only the "bright Marimekko textiles" she hung, but also the image of "six-year-old Gio"—Francis and Eleanor's son who would die a young man—"pounding nails in the wall of the new mixing studio."[124] But if American Zoetrope brought family into the workplace, in a reciprocal action it brought the workplace into the family home, once sequestered from commerce. Think, again, of Preston Tucker and the engines built on "a kitchen stove." It is no wonder that Coppola's children grew up to be filmmakers: no separation obtained between his work life and his home life, a condition that sums up the new economy for which Coppola agitated.

In this light, we ought to consider the final gesture of *The Rain People*. The movie can be interpreted as an effort to imagine new relations, but these new relations can look like a mere salvage job of old relations. In the closing scene, Officer Gordon is being battered by Killer, who had watched Gordon intend Natalie harm. The scene is an odd one, comprising the widower Gordon and his motherless daughter, also the motherless Killer, and at its center the pregnant Natalie, the object of Gordon's unrestrained lust. Broken families, in short, contend with each other outside Gordon's mobile home. It looks like Killer, true to his name, will kill Gordon, but Gordon's daughter defends her father by grabbing his state-issued handgun and shooting Killer twice in the back. He crumples. In this moment Natalie stares at Gordon's daughter, their glance lasting nearly too long, before she assumes her Pietà ministrations over Killer's body.

Some sort of relay has happened, here, between the officer's daughter and the football player's proxy mother. Formal authority has eliminated substantive authority, on the one side, and a girl has been pitted against a woman, on the other side. The law is in crisis, no doubt, as so much sixties historiography attests it was at the time, but there seems to be a Hegelian notion of the law's recalibration at work here: the family, which gives substantive authority to the state's positive law, must renew itself and recover legitimacy on another order. "I'll take care of you, I'll protect you," Natalie tells Killer. "Vinny will take care of you. I'll call him, he'll come here, and he'll take us both back." What makes the scene uncanny is that her pledge—"And we'll be a family"—is made to a corpse; yet we know all the while that Natalie is pregnant, a pregnancy she has considered terminating, and which her husband Vinny has finally given his permission for her to terminate. In this moment—on having equalized relations with her husband, on having flirted with formal law before returning to substantive authority—she affirms her commitment to family again. It might be a cop-out. Natalie may have done nothing more than emancipate herself within the middle-class structure only to make that structure more sound.

The Form of the Firm: *The Godfather,*
The Conversation, and *Tucker*

One of the more surprising leaps in any director's filmography is the one Coppola made between *The Rain People* and *The Godfather*. If *The Rain People* was concerned to recalibrate the lyric voice, and if it placed its storytelling on the order of impact of a poem, *The Godfather* was more like a realist novel, concerned with how people in their private corners are necessarily cast into relation with a great, teeming society. "Just when I thought I was out," goes the line from the last *Godfather*, "they pull me back in." The difference is appropriate enough, given the production situation of the two movies. *The Rain People* was a personal movie; *The Godfather,* a studio movie. Coppola was fond of saying that, for his own sake, he justified taking on the project—famously, *The Godfather* was offered him by Paramount when no established director would accept it—by committing to alter the type of movie it would be. He would not make a "gangster cheapie" but instead would carve from Mario Puzo's novel the more compelling "story of the family, this father and his sons, and questions of power and succession."[125] In his hands, the movie veered from the genre's staple theme of class rise and instead took on the more collective topic of American business. In paralleling mafia life and "our biggest industries," Coppola said, he meant to interrogate "corporate philosophy."[126] He shaped the material this way so that he might convert a genre movie into a personal movie. What Coppola cared about, after all, was the succession story of corporate philosophy, what the next generation would do with the firm as a figure of thought and an organizing device of capital. *The Rain People* cared about subjectivity because it aimed to disrupt the social reproduction of certain kinds of subjects on which Fordism depends. *The Godfather* took this lyric subjectivity and pressed it into the social register of opera, where one's inner voice is meaningful, and indeed gains amplitude, precisely to the extent that it is projected outward and spread over the great, teeming chorus of voices. In this sense, a formal analysis of the movie will reveal that its investment in operatic principles is the same as its concern for unity in group enterprise—or, in the language of American business, the firm. In still another sense it is imperative to see how the countercultural impulses of the era, though in Coppola's idiosyncratic case they were filtered through the art of opera first, tended to find their way back to the corporation as their object of rehabilitation. Group life, in this era, was that much defined by it.

The Rain People was on its face concerned with family structure, but behind the scenes it was concerned with business structure. The Godfather was intent instead to show no useful distinction between family and business. One of its more famous epigrams, "This is business, not personal," becomes incoherent when Michael Corleone shows that deeply personal conviction must constitute business decisions. Its thesis seems to be that such a division is arbitrary and can never hold. In this light, Coppola was able to make a certain kind of argument with the movie. What's at stake is exactly what makes a business. This question, something of a philosophical fascination for Coppola throughout his career, became one worth arguing when American Zoetrope lost its financial lifeline. Once established, the firm produced THX-1138—cheaply and quickly, as Coppola bragged—and submitted it to Warner Bros., where John Calley and Ted Ashley rejected not only the movie but the firm itself. All seven projects Coppola had brought them, including scripts for Apocalypse Now and The Conversation, were defunded. Not only that, but Calley and Ashley wanted to recuperate the advance money that Coppola had already spent in Europe on state-of-the-art sound and editing equipment. Short on capital, Zoetrope would make commercials, rent equipment, and so on. In a sense, this stage in the life of Zoetrope modulated Coppola's very notion of what made a firm: he once thought owning the "means of production" was success itself, but now those means—the cameras, editing boards, and so on—were without capital to prime them and rather less useful therefore. Owning the means, in itself, only meant that he could sell the means, or rent them as he in fact did, but the property transaction did not interest him, as it was merely incidental to the workings of a firm, whose nature, Coppola had come to see, must lie someplace else.

During this crisis, Paramount offered Coppola The Godfather. Since the project was "presold" by Mario Puzo's novel, it had a chance to be lucrative and hence return American Zoetrope to solvency. Coppola, who had cautioned his cohort against genre, first refused the offer. It fell to George Lucas to persuade him that the fate of their corporate idea rode on his directing the Paramount assignment. What happened next, everyone knows: Coppola made a movie that would gross more than any before it. This turn of the screw, alas, abets a messianic version of Hollywood history. In it, the maverick little guy defies the hidebound establishment and, in winning for himself, redeems the greater enterprise (the motion picture industry, in this case). Warner executives look foolish now, such history says, having passed on Coppola and Lucas; foolish because their passing on talent seems to scan—too easily, I'll insist—as having passed on *The Godfather* and *Star Wars*. They were so focused on money, and the known formula for making it, that they missed some of the biggest payouts in that decade's box office. An embittered Coppola gave the story this cast when, years later, he spoke of Warner's "embarrassment over the fact that all these young guys that they had abandoned were becoming successful."[127] The story, though, is more complicated and more interesting than that. Warner Bros. did pass on *Apocalypse Now,* true, though in a time well before movies were being made about Vietnam, and in a form quite unlike the one the movie took later in the decade. And they did scuttle their relationship with Coppola and Lucas, two definitive filmmakers of the 1970s. But the past is always distorted in the gotcha perspective of the present, where perfect judgment is vouched us by no longer needing to be exercised. Calley and Ashley did not, in fact, reject blockbuster movies for lack of foresight, though they did in this case lack foresight. What they rejected was a management style, and a definition of the firm, that they found unrecognizable.

Calley and Ashley were the products of what the business historian Alfred D. Chandler Jr. has called the "managerial revolution." Neither made movies. Before being named the brass at Warner Bros., Calley had worked in advertising and then produced television; Ashley had been a talent agent his whole life, first for William Morris and then for his own company, Ashley-Famous. That they had backgrounds in marketing and talent management, not moviemaking in any facet other than its deal-making side, would have struck them as right and just. In this episode of corporate history, after all, management had autonomized itself. It was a meta-skill that, through its application, could enhance and make more efficient any given business. The management credo had allowed the corporation to metastasize into its current form. Breaking the firm's dependency on a charismatic owner, management had let corporate structure subdivide into many units—what would become, under the original "company man," Alfred Sloan, the multidivisional business. Janet Staiger traces this as a local history within Hollywood when she notes the passage from the director-unit system, to the central producer system, and then into the producer-unit system. Articulated as they were, the studios surely looked like congenial structures to the corporate conglomerate. With a shift onto these ownership scales, though, the object of corporate management would no longer be movies but business divisions. The conglomerate, in this respect no more than a behemoth form of the multidivisional firm, would impose its externalized management class on Hollywood upon absorbing it. The belief carrying the day—namely, that management as such "could master any sort of unrelated business"—had the effect of confusing the project of business management and the project of the corporation as such, making the one seem a synonym for the other.[128]

Nonetheless, the corporation, legally defined, has nothing to do with diversity; it has to do, as the term suggests, with "incorporating" loose parts into a single substance. And hence nothing intrinsic to corporate form requires that management transcend the firm's varied functions and become the unitary substance. Indeed, what American Zoetrope would propose is that too narrowly business-minded an interpretation of the firm had rendered it an ineffectual form. The conglomerate, for all its economies of scale, only dilutes the identity of a brand. How American Zoetrope would oppose corporate form, and help regenerate it in doing so, is a main interest in a sequence of Coppola movies running from *The Godfather* to *The Conversation* to *Tucker*. It is worth keeping in mind that, after Warner Bros. had weakened Zoetrope as a going business concern, it survived largely as an idea; but the corporation, we might say, has lived its whole life as an idea.

The key to understanding *The Godfather*, I propose, and in particular the romance it finds in family self-sufficiency and informal economy, is to return it to the problem of the sixties from which, as a period piece, it seems to exempt itself. On this note, we might compare it to *Patton*, a Coppola screenplay that likewise refracted present history through the past. *Patton* is a document of official culture, *The Godfather* a repudiation of it. When the latter movie opens on Bonasera in full face, he is being upbraided by the Don for the shameful position in which his overconfidence in official culture has left him. "You had a good trade, you made a good living," Don Corleone says. "The police protected you, and there were courts of law." But when Bonasera needs justice, he finds it miscarried by its would-be impartial officers. Official culture is corrupt, in short, because its officers make it personal: they ethnicize civil rights, say, when they ought to universalize them. It could never be otherwise, the Don thinks, self-interest being so basic to the desire for law in the first place.

This theme is central to *Patton,* too, in that General Patton was committed to personal style, as his pearl-handled revolvers attest. Coppola claims that the likeable side of Patton that he pushed forward, to offset his vicious side, was his being a "literary" southern gentleman. In other words, Patton was an anachronism in the armies of an administered society because he was driven by feudal personality in a time when only impersonal procedure was thought able to run large-scale operations. Central as that may be to *Patton* and *The Godfather,* a more telling comparison lies in the formal decision to begin both movies with direct addresses of the camera. Like Bonasera, Patton faces the camera and delivers his oration to an audience outside the frame. His address seems directed, audaciously enough, at us, the spectators. In important senses, though, there are greater differences than similarities between Bonasera and Patton: Bonasera beseeches the audience while Patton hails it; Bonasera has learned he is never more than an immigrant, hence always an outsider in America, while Patton considers it his duty to decide what qualifies someone as an American ("All real Americans," he says, "love the sting of battle"); and Bonasera, for these reasons, is experiencing a crisis of faith in America, while Patton has no doubt about it. The difference between the two, in effect, marks the transition from self-certainty about the American project to self-doubt about it. This, in other language, has been called the end of consensus.

These two opening scenes overlay each other in significant ways. In the late 1960s, in the thick of the Vietnam War, both movies fend off the contemporary moment and opt to set their stories in a historical past. Coppola insisted on setting *The Godfather* in the immediate post–World War II period. When Mario Puzo adapted the novel, he had made its setting contemporary, "complete with references to hippies."[129] Coppola, however, pushed it back to the postwar moment and

General Patton directly addresses the camera.

made its opening scene a nod to *Patton,* because in some crucial way the opening scene of the new movie, *The Godfather,* needed to overlay the Prussian militarism and consensus politics of General Patton's World War II. Michael Corleone, after all, gets his training in Patton's war. Michael will turn out to be a failed product of the postwar consensus, as it were, because he stops accepting the ideology of what has been called Military Keynesianism—the comfortable arrangement between wartime industry and the state that had been the driver of American prosperity. "Senator Corleone, Governor Corleone," the Don had wished for his son, Michael. "Another *pezzonovante,*" Michael says, suggesting that his father's wish to formalize the family's success is more shameful than keeping it informal as they have. A *pezzonovante* needs a recognized office to draw undue power in service of his own projects. Michael doubts this structure. He is the voice from *within* the structure, casting doubt on it. This is the relevance, finally, of his "nice Ivy League suit" and his military decorations. It makes frustration with the system internal to it. Consider this within the context of a remark made by Michael Rossman, an organizer in Berkeley's Free Speech Movement (FSM). "Somewhere in the process of the FSM," Rossman says, "the young, privileged, affluent children of the culture began to see themselves as an oppressed class." Those "destined to be the managers of the society," he says, were the ones rejecting the terms on which it ran.[130]

Michael Corleone might seem remote from Berkeley student protests in the 1960s, but this is only the strategic effect Coppola got from pushing the movie's historical setting back two decades. Michael is remote from sixties youth, in consequence, but he still needs to be seen in relation to them. To give this connection its due force, we ought to consider another episode in the lengthy wedding scene that opens *The Godfather*. After Bonasera, the next guest to petition the Don is the baker, Nazorine. He asks the Don to stop the deportation of his assistant, Enzo, who had been granted status as a guest worker in behalf of the "American war effort" but was now being repatriated to Italy. The theme of transition from wartime to peacetime economy is thus marked. Underscoring it, the movie cuts from the Don inside his office to an exterior shot of Michael in soldier's uniform entering the wedding party with Kay (Diane Keaton) on his arm. The cut associates Michael and Enzo, as young men starting careers in the postwar economy, and the association is not strictly incidental; it's reinforced in a later scene when Michael and Enzo stand abreast on the steps of the hospital, making their best show of force against the machinery of the state—namely, the corrupt police officer McCluskey, who has in his own interest denied Don Corleone the police protection to which he is entitled. What is thrilling in this scene is that Michael, finding his father unguarded in his hospital room, puts together a show of force through the scant means available, an altogether impromptu act on his part, and the show of force, though fake, is successful. "Get rid of these," Michael says of Enzo's flowers, and by popping Enzo's coat collar he transforms him from baker into gangster. "Put your hand in your pocket like you have a gun," Michael instructs him. The scene stages the de facto transition of Corleone family authority from father to son, with Vito on oxygen upstairs and Michael down below reanimating his father's power catch-as-catch-can.

Michael, in this sense, is an anachronistic expression of the counterculture's frustration with the crony capitalism and state-driven enterprises ensured in the arrangement that President Eisenhower would call the military-industrial complex. If we flash forward to *The Godfather, Part II*, which is to say to the mature phase of Michael's leadership, we see that the first object of the narrative's comeuppance is Senator Geary, a senator the audience is ostensibly meant to oppose because he uses racist grounds for denying Michael fair terms for a gaming license. Like Patton, Geary would define the "real American," and in Geary's case this definition is no more than an updating of the Progressive-era defense of Anglo-Saxon ethnicity as the soul of American identity. His racism, however, might give us no more than an alibi for our other reason to hate him while reserving sympathy for Michael. After all, the Corleone family is not innocent of racism, and hence the audience isn't likely to elevate Michael above Senator Geary on these grounds. The affective mechanics that solicit our respect for Michael but our disrespect for Geary are rooted in the official sanction that Geary enjoys but Michael does not. Official culture is held in contempt because it impinges on Michael's economic freedom.

Indeed, Jon Lewis suggests that the movie's contemporary audiences related to Michael not strictly because he fell on the youthful side of a generation gap the movie was addressing—a prominent theme in this period Hollywood, notably worked out in *The Graduate* (1967)—but because he "usher[ed] in a new, more modern way of doing business."[131] This is roughly true, so long as it doesn't turn into a proleptic description of future audiences who would celebrate the new business credo in a figure like Gordon Gecko (Michael Douglas) from *Wall Street* (1987). Michael, in this view, would be an early rendering of the businessman aggrandized for his greed and ruthlessness. David Thompson later makes such a claim, noting that the executives for whom Michael's influence was most enduring were those in Hollywood industry.[132] What constrains him in the role of *homo economicus,* however, must be understood in relation not to the future moment of Reaganomics, nor to the past moment of postwar optimism, which is to say to the diegetic moment of the movie, but rather to the moment of Coppola's early career, the New Hollywood. In this moment, while Hollywood tried clinging to tradition, it seemed that everywhere else there were radical denunciations of the state and "the system" being sounded by members of the New Left.[133] If SDS's Carl Oglesby, say, represented a more disaffected view of America's political system as an "inner oligarchic power sphere" that had the CIA contract "its skills out to ITT to destroy democracy's last little chance in Chile"—and it's worth noting that, when Coppola claims violence as part of legitimate business, he uses ITT as his example—then its more mainstream critics, such as Richard Kaufman in the *New York Times Magazine,* decried it for placing in check the competition that he deems the main engine of capitalism.[134] In Coppola's moment, the senators and their appropriations, the Department of Defense and its contracts, and

Ominously, Senator Geary represents white Anglo-Saxon official culture.

the corporations and their lobbies were fixed in an official arrangement that was corrupt enough to deserve whatever undoing it got. Imagined from this perspective, the senator had, *ex officio,* earned the audience's disrespect.

Before we consider what the movie is offering in place of official culture, we should look at the scene in the first *Godfather* that holds roughly the same structural place Senator Geary's episode does in the second movie. This is the scene with Jack Woltz (John Marley), the studio boss at Woltz Pictures. The movies are structured in roughly the same way, with the important exception that the second movie intercalates the story of Vito's ascendancy into the story of the established family. The first *Godfather* opens on the wedding of Vito's daughter, with Vito carrying on business throughout, and the second opens on the first communion of Michael's son, with Michael likewise discharging business all the while. Where Michael's business is an intransigent senator, Vito's had been an intransigent studio boss. Johnny Fontaine, Vito's godson, could not get a movie part he is "perfect for," according to Woltz, who for personal reasons wants to "run him out of the business." It's personal, too, for Senator Geary, who says, "I don't like your kind of people." The language Geary uses ("your oily hair, dressed up in your silk suits") echoes Woltz's ("with his olive oil voice and guinea charm");

their scenes of comeuppance, in turn, mirror each other, with Woltz waking in bloody sheets, a severed horse head buried within, and Geary waking with a dead prostitute, the texture of bloody sheets once again being the lurid visual effect. What needs to be remarked in these rhyming scenes is that we start in the Hollywood industry and move beyond to the more recognized arena of official culture, American politics; in this movement we trace the itinerary of Coppola and Lucas's project, which took Hollywood as its first object of reform but would necessarily reconstitute its object of critique as Keynesian economy at large. This, despite their being apolitical otherwise.

What needs to be stressed now is that Coppola made *The Godfather* in between the establishment of two businesses, American Zoetrope and the Director's Company, which gives the movie the peculiar status of being a lacuna in Coppola's experiments with corporate identity. He was, for *The Godfather,* a director-for-hire. Making the movie gave him a chance to cope with, and process, what seemed the failure of American Zoetrope and to consider what exactly constitutes business success. In his next movie, *The Conversation,* Coppola had a greater degree of independence, or at least it would look that way: he shot on location in his adopted city, San Francisco, and for a subsidiary firm in which he had an executive share, the Director's Company.

The following discussion charts, on the one hand, a progression within Coppola's movies in how the firm, *qua* idea, is represented, hence making for a highly localized intellectual history of the corporation in the 1970s; and it registers, on the other hand, just how sensitive the form-content admixture of Coppola's movies was to the companies that authorized their making. It progresses through *The Godfather,* a movie about family business; *The Conversation,* a movie about an owner-operated business; and *Tucker,* a movie that averages both these business structures, and as such becomes a movie about how a discourse of the firm has regulated what business can do. The discussion requires three steps. First, I offer detailed readings of scenes from *The Godfather* to show what seems to be a refinement in Coppola's concept of the corporation. Next, I consider how the paranoia of *The Conversation* makes sense in light of the intellectual compromise with Paramount that the Director's Company proved to be. And finally, I analyze *Tucker* in formal terms to understand what has been called Coppola's postmodernism, on display there and in the sequence including *One from the Heart* and *Rumble Fish* (1983). What counts as "postmodernism" in this series is a tendency, both instantiated and critiqued within the movies, for signifying practices to subsume the processes of production and warp them in doing so.

Family Capital

For *The Godfather* Coppola needed an additional tête-à-tête between Vito and Michael that would fill out their relationship, but never having found time to write the scene, he famously farmed it out to the screenwriter Robert Towne. This is the scene in which Vito confesses to Michael his unrealized hope to have legitimized the family business via Michael's installation in official culture. What needs remarking is not simply the scene's narrative function but its structural function. While the father-son relationship is here more fully characterized, it is done by spoken means. By this I don't mean only that it is dialogue-set exposition. Rather, it is a bit of spoken connective tissue between the more extravagant set pieces that the movie uses elsewhere to convey information. I want to suggest that by putting this scene in relation to others, we will understand how the principles of opera give the movie its form. This spoken exposition, a respite from the dramatic pitch, bears to the set pieces elsewhere the same relation we find in the recitative (singing patterned on ordinary speech) and aria (singing structured by expressive melody) in opera.

The recitative scenes in *The Godfather* give shape and texture to the social ties between characters; its arias show moments in which characters try to extricate themselves from, and lift themselves above, social ties. The ariatic moments, such as Michael's stand at the hospital or Sonny's murder at the toll booths, are grand displays of voice, provided we understand voice in cinema in terms of visual demonstration. These arias do depend on the dimension of sound, potentially even on the score as such, but their quality of expressive voice is better described as a fusion of audiovisual design. Consider, for instance, Sonny's aria, which I'll mark as beginning with his sister, Connie, answering a phone call from her husband's mistress. The scene begins with an empty, black frame, over which we hear the shrill ring of the phone. The phone's ring introduces the refrain of strident noise that will mark time throughout this aria. It will be relayed, next, through Connie and Carlo's screaming match, the cacophony of Connie breaking dishes, the slapping of Carlo's belt strap, and then a jump in location, from Connie's apartment to the Corleone home, cut together by Connie's scream transferring to a baby's scream, as Sonny takes Connie's phone call. Then, the near white noise of car tires grinding around a gravel drive, followed by the excessive rat-a-tat machine-gun fire at the toll booths, and then the final rise of all this cacophony into the melody of Nino Rota's theme. The tight design of this passage is revealed not only in sound design, but in the editing pattern, which throughout Connie and Carlo's fight is carefully staged in sequence shots, cut together, at points of emphasis, by countershots and orchestrated camera distances.

The careful design of this passage, we soon realize, mimics the careful design of the plot: Carlo had it all planned, his beating Connie and her bidding Sonny's defense, which would place Sonny at the toll booth at the designated hour, where Carlo had sold out Sonny to the Barzini family. Properly speaking, this should be called the Connie-Sonny aria, because it casts in balletic form what we might call the agonistic bond of family of which Connie and Sonny are the avatars. Family is affirmed, for them, in scenes of violent love. Sonny will expose himself when he turns to violently avenge his sister's injury. Sonny, therefore, could only die a violent death, its gruesomeness in exact proportion to the charge

Sonny's aria.

of his emotional life. This passage, to put a fine point on it, needs to be understood as an expressively saturated mode of characterization in counterpoint to the mode of characterization—the recitative, as it were—carried out in ordinary speech. The former is, finally, the ordinary life of the latter raised to the condition of music.

Interesting, in this context, is the fact that the Connie-Sonny aria was shot as it was because the Paramount executive Robert Evans, feeling that there was too little action in the movie, had threatened to send an "action director" to deliver the scene. Coppola and Evans were often at odds, and they have kept up hostilities over the years. But let's entertain the possibility that Evans suggested more "action" not to harass the young Coppola but on the intuition that, in a movie so symmetrical— weighted at both ends with ceremonies—the Connie-Sonny set piece was structurally necessary as the counterpart scene to Michael's set piece at the hospital: in one aria, Michael ascends; in the other, Sonny falls. The one complements, and indeed explains, the other. Sonny falls because he too rashly arrogates the family's voice. He tries not to, by biting his fist as though, like a cartoon character, he might bottle up the voice, but his incapacity to mete out his words is part of his nature. Michael rises on just this capacity. And his set piece at the hospital, though it is predicated on his capacity for decisive action, is marked by the theme of regulated speech. When Officer McCluskey arrives, Michael asks him, "What's the Turk paying you to set up my father, Captain?" McCluskey then punches Michael and breaks his jaw. After this, Michael speaks differently, his voice trained by a clenched jaw for only the most necessary use. His cheek is swollen, at first, such that he resembles his father, Vito, whom Marlon Brando famously gave bulldog cheeks by stuffing them with tissues in his screen test.[135] And even as Michael's swelling goes down, he shows a bruise there throughout his stay in Sicily, which attests that his jawbone has been restructured. Michael inherits the voice of the family, in other words, only on the condition that he be pained to use it wantonly.

In this light, we can think of the tête-à-tête between Vito and Michael as the structural complement to another recitative scene, the one in which Vito does business with Sollozzo in the office of his olive oil company. This scene outlines not only how the family does business, but more fundamentally what counts *as a business* in the first place.

Michael's broken jaw is proof that he has restraint enough to use the family voice.

Crucially, it is all routed through the exercise of voice. What is outlined is the form of the firm. The firm, as theorized here, is not strictly a matter of voice; it is a matter of how the voice is given a transpersonal and, indeed, a family structure. The scene begins with a canny edit. In the preceding scene, Vito had been at home in consultation with Tom and Sonny, planning their response to the backing Sollozzo requested of them. This scene of the family home, however, is intercut with scenes of Sollozzo's arrival at Vito's office. As Tom profiles Sollozzo, it flashes forward to their eventual meeting with him but then cuts back to the Corleone home in parallel fashion. The effect is to interpenetrate not only the temporalities of the planning and execution of business but also the spaces of home and business. It gives us to understand that the family plans its business style before acting it out. The home consultation concludes with Sonny asking the Don, "So what's your answer gonna be, Pop?" And though we have little doubt that he shares it with them, the movie conceals his answer from us, for the moment, by way of a contemplative rest from Vito and a cut to Sollozzo now in the Don's office. The cut creates suspense, of course—whether Vito will move the family into the drug racket is deferred—but it also makes a point of Vito's silence. He will not speak in anything but a unitary voice, and only when addressed by Sollozzo and in view of the gathered family.

And the Don speaks in very deliberate tones ("I must say no to you," he says, "and I'll give you my reasons").

Carefully considered, we can see in this modest scene the outlines of the movie's overall formal and thematic strategies. While Vito speaks on behalf of the family, he does so in what first appears to be an individual agon between himself and Sollozzo. This is formally signaled by a shot-countershot pattern that alternates medium close-ups of Sollozzo and Vito. Only when Vito asks Sollozzo about the interest of the Tattaglia family does the shot pattern break to include, by way of Sollozzo's eyeline acknowledgment, a medium close-up of Tom. "My compliments," toasts Sollozzo, thereby showing that whatever Vito says is underwritten by the research and the cunning of the entire family. The shot-countershot pattern of medium close-ups, however, is only broken by a long shot—and a long shot that finally reveals that Vito is flanked by family—when he stands and readies to deliver his answer. What this form tells us is that the work of many, by some odd calculation, must find articulation in the voice of one.

This is the form of the firm, and it is thematically explicated, in short order, by Sonny's seemingly uncalculated objection to Sollozzo, "Are you telling me that the Tattaglias will guarantee our investment?" Sonny has not been authorized to speak, we understand, and when he does he reveals that the thin justification for the firm is its defense against exposure to the interests of the marketplace. The economist Ronald Coase had famously explained the emergence of the firm in just these terms. Coase argued against the orthodoxy that the price mechanism alone organized the "economic system," explaining instead that what marks the firm is the "supersession of the price mechanism" by another relation—an internal rather than external relation.[136] We can call this internal relation "hierarchy." Sonny at once recognizes a solecism in Sollozzo's promise that the Corleone million will be guaranteed by the Tattaglias. Sollozzo is saying something confused: the Tattaglias, though entering a market contract, are willing to extend their internal protections to an external party, the Corleones. It sounds like a world without risk, where the protections of the family extend endlessly throughout society—where the seam between one family and another, that is, never shows. However, internalizing costs—constituting a firm, in other words—is undertaken explicitly in response to the costs incurred outside in a radically uncentered and unpredictable marketplace. Sonny gets this, it seems, but in a crucial way he doesn't get how the firm must act. The firm acts as a unified aggregate, as a "lump of butter coagulating in a pail of buttermilk," in the effort to deny the randomizing effects of atomistic markets.[137] When Sonny speaks without authorization, he is meeting the market on its terms and, in turn, annulling the form of order raised against it. He isolates himself as an individual—"Never tell anybody outside the family what you're thinking again," the Don reprimands him—and he will be sacrificed therefore.

Much as this delineates the form of the firm, it is hard to overlook that in *The Godfather* it's a family, not a firm. This, Fredric Jameson has argued, is the movie's "utopian function."[138] It redescribes business in terms of "family itself."[139] Against contemporary anxieties that late capitalism had eroded the family bond, Jameson says that "the ethnic group can seem to project an image of social reintegration by way of the patriarchal and authoritarian family of the past."[140] The ethnic identity of the Corleones is arguably what makes their family seem close-knit next to, say, Senator Geary's family of convenience (he visits prostitutes for pleasure, we infer, but has a wife for professional appearances). This is a fair take on the movie, but Jameson perhaps mistakenly deems this recourse to family strictly an ideological sop when in fact it was, in Coppola's case, something more like pragmatic advice for Hollywood conglomerates. The insight is basic enough: the hierarchy of internal relation seems noncompulsory when described in terms of family rather than business. A parent is different from a boss, because a parent's support is not tied to one's performance. Hegel called this an ethical relation in its "immediate phase," which is to say it happens without the mediation of an outside party such as the state.[141] Employment relations, by contrast, were thusly mediated; a legal history attends them. Coppola needed to turn back the clock to gain this insight, not because it derived from a chapter of mafia history but rather from early stages of corporate history.

For the business historian Alfred D. Chandler Jr., this insight animates the "personal capitalism" that set late nineteenth- and early twentieth-century British firms apart from their American and German counterparts.[142] British firms did not, on balance, develop a management class as did American and German firms. Instead they were "personally managed," Chandler explains, which means that the owner of the company also managed operations, and because it is biologically impossible for the founder of a concern to manage it in perpetuity, management of a firm would be extended through the family.[143] In an important sense, this makes the legal notion of corporate personhood intelligible, as the "person" can still be construed in biological terms and legally anchored by what Hegel calls "family capital." As an example of the British family firm, Chandler cites Cadbury Brothers, Ltd. Long a family-run firm, Cadbury is a useful reference point for Coppola's latter-day designs on a corporate utopia. The Cadbury brothers relocated their factory outside the urban center of Birmingham and planned open-air houses and recreational areas for workers that would come to be known as a "factory in a garden."[144] The Cadbury brothers were utopians, in short, who based their company's moral "ethos" in their Quaker beliefs.[145] Limned in this precedent, one can already see Mogens Skot-Hansen's bucolic production facilities that would one day inspire Coppola's blueprint for American Zoetrope, flung far, as it would be, from the industrial quick of Hollywood. For an example closer to home, one might consider Walt Disney's Hyperion Avenue studio, which represents the halcyon moment when the Disney Company was still run on a family ethos, with Walt involved in every phase, before the firm expanded and faced the 1941 labor strikes that would signal the company's new juridical character.

The examples pile up. We might find one in Zoetrope's contemporary, BBS Productions, a Columbia small unit run by Bert Schneider, son of Columbia president Abe Schneider. In view of these examples, we have occasion to see how *The Godfather* can be indexed to a historical imaginary of the corporation. Of equal importance, we might consider *The Godfather* trilogy an interested survey of the historical vicissitudes of the family firm: how it is, for instance, that the family idea is at risk of being penetrated and organized altogether by business values. Business must be run like family, in other words, but family cannot be run like business. This is the lesson that *The Godfather, Part II* carries. It is a critique of the various skewings to which Hegel's family dialectic is historically vulnerable. Even in Hegel, the equilibrated state in which a "family becomes one person and its members become its accidents" is thrown off by a situation in which women enjoy "substantiality" only in "inward life" and not in "full actualization."[146] Men, by contrast, do enjoy their wills becoming actualized substance in "the state" (i.e. in public life).[147]

This occluded dialectic—at the level of the family, but thence contaminating society at every level—is what *The Rain People* had meant to redress. But in the closing shot of *The Godfather*, we see that Michael has hijacked the family idea: in barring Kay from his office, he has taken what fell to him as the Corleone identity, short-circuited any progressive logic within it, and plunged it back into a bygone era. This is why, we can now assert, the second *Godfather* is narrated within a historical perspective: we see the feudal warlords of Sicily on one end, and the guerilla rebels of Havana on the other end. Michael is wary of the rebels because their fellowship, unified in the name of Cuban autonomy, raises them to another order of force. "They can win," he says of the rebels, because "the soldiers are paid to fight, the rebels aren't." In short, money is weak incentive. This is true not only for an army but also for a business. Vito Corleone understood this, seemingly, for he declined Sollozzo's offer of easy money in the name of his business identity. "It's true I have a lot of friends in politics," he conceded, "but they wouldn't be friendly very long if they knew my business was drugs instead of gambling." He guarded the family's business identity, on the one hand, while he protected it from the distortions of the profit motive on the other hand. It is no surprise that Coppola should use Cuba's situation to make this point. The bottom-up spirit of their revolution, after all, looks much like Zoetrope's business model. After studying Cuba for the movie, Coppola later visited and was impressed. "In terms of this new culture," Coppola said of Cuba, "the first thing I started to see is that the people seemed to be wired together in a singularity of purpose . . . everyone is connected to some *idea* and that makes people feel good."[148] We see in Coppola's future movies a sober recognition that the idea of a bottom-up ethos, in business as in politics, will often be exploited as the *appearance* of an enterprise—everyone likes the terms "democracy" and "autonomy"—even after its *substance* is lost.

The Paranoid Style in Corporate History

This lesson gathers its force in the formation of the Directors Company, a corporate entity that called up the appearance of Zoetrope but none of its substance. And the lesson is given form in *The Conversation*, the lone movie Coppola would make for the company. Per agreement, the Directors Company would have had him deliver more movies. However, the Directors Company, as Peter Bart has put it most laconically, "was never really a company."[149] The narrative of its formation sounds different depending on who tells it. Jon Lewis describes it as the "brainchild" of Frank Yablans, Paramount's president, whereas Michael Schumacher credits the initiative to the Gulf and Western CEO (and, thereby, Paramount's owner) Charles Bluhdorn, who felt that Hollywood's underclassmen, a.k.a. the movie brats, had "graduated from making arty, film-school movies to the more grown-up world of big commercial pictures."[150] In this latter scenario, Yablans was largely the public front for a project authorized above him. The project, no matter its long-term success, is an interesting one, particularly for the perspective in which it places Coppola's business philosophy.

In 1972 Paramount deputized Coppola and his fellow directors Peter Bogdanovich and William Friedkin as the heads of an autonomous production unit within the larger studio. "Under the initial plan," Bart explains, "the three were not only free to choose their projects (within certain budgetary limits), but could also exercise complete creative control. Moreover, each could name a youthful 'protégé' who would also make a film for the company."[151] If one were to ask why *these three* directors, the answer would be as simple as recent box-office tallies: *The Godfather, The Last Picture Show* (dir. Bogdanovich, 1969), and *The French Connection* (dir. Friedkin, 1971). The company was formed, in short, on the misguided notion that these three filmmakers shared the goal of crafting their generation's sensibility into some commercially viable new cinema. This might describe Friedkin's ambition. He worried from the start, Bart recalls, "about the projects his colleagues were selecting" and personally "favored more commercial fare."[152] But Bogdanovich meant less to channel a new sensibility than an old one, namely Orson Welles's: when he brought Bart his "protégé," indeed, it was Welles (not at all "youthful"), and when Welles suggested he read Henry James's *Daisy Miller*, Bogdanovich made it his next movie for the company.

Coppola, in contrast, was concerned less with a new cinema than he was with the business unit that would allow its making. When taken as a statement on career-making, *The Conversation* attests to the kinds of distortion a business idea is vulnerable to once the source of its motivation changes. We should bear in mind that *The Conversation* was part of the slate of movies Zoetrope sold to Warner Bros. as the original future of their firm. That original future mutated, of course, and in turn the Zoetrope version of *The Conversation* was never made. When Coppola signed on for *The Godfather,* Paramount had to pay Warner Bros. the money it had not recouped from Coppola. The effect was that Coppola now owned this slate of movies once more, and his filmography, in between *Godfather* commitments, would be dedicated to producing Zoetrope's ideas—its future, as it were—under different corporate signs. And under the sign of the Directors Company, *The Conversation* became a curious treatise on the reason for doing one's job. The reason for doing one's job, it declares, is not to deny but to affirm one's connectedness to people, but the "singularity of purpose," or the source of connectedness, cannot be money. This is why *The Conversation* thematizes prostitution as a binding double of work life.

Coppola prefers to analogize work and prostitution not in moralistic suspicion of either but rather as a prescription for adding love to make each bearable. "That's being a prostitute, in a way, when you're making films as a job," he says. "But if I were a prostitute, I would only spend the night with someone I could find something to fall in love with."[153] The limitations of this analogy notwithstanding, it works as thematic infrastructure for *The Conversation.* In it, Harry Caul (Gene Hackman) is among the best in the field of surveillance, perhaps the best "bar none," as his competitor Bernie Moran tells him. He is self-employed, an owner-operator, and while the opening scenes of the movie suggest that others work for him, it seems they do so on a job-by-job basis. Stan (John Cazale) is his assistant, but that doesn't last. The logic of the material requires that Harry and Stan cannot be bound in a lasting work relationship. For Harry there is scarcely any form of internal relation, such as is constitutive of a family or corporation; he knows only external relation, vouched in money and hence abrogated as easily as any sales transaction. In his case, therefore, everything outside the self is available only in the act of prostitution. In some sense, this is Coppola's most pragmatic statement on working not only in Hollywood but in capitalist society more generally. The point of the movie is to caution against mere pragmatism as the grounds for doing one's work. Harry, in committing absolutely to a model of work organized by money, must fend off paranoia as the upshot of these beliefs. Were he to remain an economic individual—pragmatically attuned to the money relation rather than ideally insulated by the corporate relation (this being the force of the movie's argument)—then Harry would plunge irretrievably into a paranoiac condition, in the effort to guard himself from others and them from him.

Consider the scene in which Harry visits his girlfriend, Amy (Teri Garr). Amy is, it seems, the closest Harry has to a personal relationship, but the salient point of the scene is that Harry pays her rent. He is a john, by the logic outlined above, and this means that it is not a personal relationship but a professional one like the rest. What this scene draws forth, though, is the paranoia that is the simple corollary of Harry's fastidious effort to keep the personal and the professional separate. Though it would seem that Harry and Amy have an ongoing affair, she knows nothing about him: not his job, not his residence, nor even that her not having his phone number is a result of him (allegedly) not owning a phone. Amy learns that this, the day of his visit, is Harry's birthday and suggests that it might hence be occasion for her discovering "something personal" about him. Their relationship, such that it is, comes off—rather awkwardly, in fact—as the staging of a counterfactual: what if we void the most personal of our interactions of their personal content altogether and replace them instead with professional imperatives? What would a relationship be like if we knew absolutely nothing about our partner? This scene suggests that the vigilance needed for keeping apart the personal and professional would leave one always paranoid that they were merging behind one's back. When Amy sings, "Wake up, you sleepyhead," her offhanded choice seems to Harry filled with cosmic design: the song is the same one sung by the subject of his surveillance, and now this unknowable fact of his professional life is known by Amy, as though she has access to his headspace, which should be, Harry thinks, his last impregnable space. In the moment, we might think Harry is losing his grasp, that the labyrinth constructed around his private self will now disintegrate, piece by piece. Indeed, this is one way to interpret the plot as it unfolds from this scene. This, however, is a weak interpretation, focused only on the movie's investment in generic protocols—its noirish treatment of privacy, urban space, and their volatile combination—but unconcerned with the stakes involved in Coppola's using the genre. The stakes, I contend, are those of one's labor. The counterfactual has been staged to show that the *reductio ad absurdum* brought about by conducting one's personal life in professional terms will equally be brought about if one bars personal feeling from professional life.

The lesson Harry learns here—that one can remain indifferent in neither personal nor professional life—is confirmed in the subsequent plot. Harry leaves Amy's that night with a newfound disregard for the propriety of personal and professional spaces. What his work has concerned, at this juncture in the plot, is the making of surveillance tapes of a young couple enmeshed in a conspiracy about which Harry knows nothing. They could be adulterous. They could soon be murdered. He has no knowledge, since the limits of his assignment are, quite simply, to make a recording. His assistant Stan asks, "Who's interested in these two anyway?" Harry answers that he doesn't know and admonishes Stan for needing to be "entertained" by—i.e. *interested in*—the job at hand. The interest lies elsewhere, Harry believes, with those paying for the job. Harry assures Stan that he doesn't care what the couple is saying; he only wants "a nice, fat recording." He defines himself, at this stage, as a technician. But his visit to Amy's signals a change in his self-conception. When Amy asks Harry about his job, he tells her he is "kind of a musician, a freelance musician." In the moment we might write this off as part of a ruse to deprive her of personal connection with him, but the movie is intent on us taking Harry's claim at face value. We know this because in the next scene, he enters an office high-rise that, in all its modernist chic, we are meant to associate with corporate rationality. When confronted with the firm's impersonal protocols—a secretary who will receive his delivery—Harry resists, "No, I'm supposed to hand it to him personally." Even the director's assistant, who tenders Harry his fifteen-thousand-dollar compensation, is too impersonal a proxy. He refuses the money, keeping the tapes instead. Harry resists the depersonalization of his work at the hands of this large, seemingly unknowable capital structure. The reason, we come to see, is that his work has effects, as his past has taught him, and he needs to control them. He prefers to relate to his work, in short, as an artist, not as a technician.

Harry Caul in the impersonal settings
of the corporation.

His status as a technician will come to seem more disingenuous than his self-description as a musician. He has always cared about his work, it turns out, but the liability this posed—a family was killed, we learn, due to his work—led him to suppress any personal feeling in his professional labor. "It had nothing to do with me," he says of the murders. "What they do with the tapes is their own business." But Harry left New York after this job, suggesting that his personal implication made it impossible for him to continue working there. His guilt now pervades his dreams. "I'm not afraid of death," Harry says in a dream sequence, "but I am afraid of murder." Much like the earlier staging of a counterfactual, the murder that is the outcome of Harry's work is part of the film's rhetorical strategy: a hyperbolic way to imagine work as an expression of one's connected-ness to others. If the way you performed your work sentenced people to death, that is, would you continue to perform your work in that way? The same was imagined in *The Godfather,* when it supposed that the liability in exercising transpersonal power (that exercised by presidents and senators, say) must be construed in terms of people being allowed to live. "Presidents and senators don't have men killed," Kay says. "Oh? Who's being naïve, Kay?"

What seems to hold interest for Coppola is not the probable truth of such claims but their rhetorical effect. And in *The Conversation,* the plot remains murky, noirishly aloof, so that its argument might be advanced more bluntly. At no time is it stated more directly than in its second, most unmistakable act of prostitution. Because Harry will not tender the tapes (i.e. his work) to the firm, its officers must hire a woman to seduce them away from him. Meredith hangs around Harry's workspace after a party, and though things had been festive there only moments earlier, Harry's thoughts are again dominated by his work. He listens to the tapes once more, analyzing their content as a student of music might a difficult composition. "She's frightened," he says of the recorded conversation, plainly concerned for the subject of his surveillance. "Forget it," Meredith says, "it's only a trick. A job. You're not supposed to feel anything about it, you're just supposed to do it—that's all." She then turns her own trick, sleeping with Harry and stealing his tapes, making her at once the femme fatale of this noir tale and the avatar of its demonized "white-collar" soullessness. We know to associate her with the ethos of the organization man and the scientifically managed corporation; the movie has told us to. Meredith had worked in New York, she says, first as a receptionist, then as a secretary, then as a "gal Friday," and finally as a "special assistant to the boss, and then I married him": telescoped in Meredith's character is Hollywood's satiric outlook on corporate hierarchy, from *His Girl Friday* (1940) to *The Apartment* (1960), wherein women do menial work for the firm so that they can marry money, and men advance in the firm so that their power can attract pretty women.

Harry, we understand, works for different reasons. He studies his work as an artist would because it involves his whole person. His claim to being a "freelance musician" means, simply, that he has an affective relationship with his work; he is not alienated from its effects. This fact is conveyed in more ways than one. Coppola's movie, it's often recalled, was inspired by Michelangelo Antonioni's *Blow-Up* (1966), in the main lines of its plot, anyway, and perhaps too in its core philosophical concern. Antonioni's movie had depicted a photographer, Thomas, who alternates between commercial and artistic work—fashion photography for-hire, and social documentation for himself—and who in the course of his work is forced to reconsider what his medium can bear. The still image, Thomas learns, imperfectly discloses the truth of a situation. In order to frame an ontological disquisition on the medium, Antonioni had begun and ended his movie with a mime troupe. The mimes recall early motion pictures for us, and the way the subtraction of sound threw the medium into a productive dependency on the visual dimension. Consider how Thomas, when in the final scenes he plays along with the mimes, begins to add sensory details where there are none: an invisible tennis ball nonetheless produces a sound. The mimes hence bookend an inquiry of another kind into the ontological difference between still and moving images (Thomas's pictures and Antonioni's picture).

In *The Conversation,* Coppola riffs on this structure in a manner so subtle that it risks passing our notice. The movie begins with a zoom-in on Union Square, the site of "the conversation," but the site too of pedestrian traffic eclectic enough to motivate the appearance of both a mime and a jazz band. Here, the mime merely evokes Antonioni, but it does not appear again in the end. Rather, the jazz becomes this movie's bookends. In the final shot, Harry, now aware that he himself is under surveillance ("The bugger got bugged," as Bernie Moran quips), sits in the corner and plays saxophone for the agents of the firm listening, he presumes, on the other end. In short, the medium is deployed—in Coppola's movie—to unsettle what had been a neat divide between private and public space. "There is no moment between two human be-ings," Moran had boasted, "that I cannot record." And the conflation of private-public—when Fordist labor had turned on their separation (i.e. you are off duty or on the clock)—is now recast as the professionalization

Harry Caul plays sax for his corporate audience.

of one's personal life. Harry's final act of defiance is performed on the self-expressive instrument par excellence, the saxophone: he renders the firm his art, no remuneration needed. The statement, of course, is that Harry works from his own motivation, not theirs.

What remains to be answered, then, is if the movie proffers this rather utopian idea of unalienated labor, why it does so in such a paranoid milieu? The movie carries a paranoid ground tone, I contend, because it registers a failure to coordinate personal projects with the corporate project. It is the failure of the Directors Company that *The Conversation* foretells, a failure that is but an epiphenomenon of the original failure of American Zoetrope. On the fate of the Directors Company, Coppola has said, "There was disagreement between us and Paramount," and "the reason we ultimately liquidated it was because Paramount never really wanted there to be a company with the autonomy that we wanted."[154] Paramount did not want to trust Coppola and his colleagues, Bogdanovich and Friedkin; it only wanted rights to their most profitable movies. It did not want to extend these directors protection under its financial aegis, as Coppola saw it; it only wanted versions of them alienated in their products. *The Godfather* mattered. *The French Connection* (1971) mattered. Harry's tapes mattered. But Coppola, Friedkin, and Harry did not. Harry's efforts, if interpreted from Coppola's standpoint, should be coordinated internally (in a corporation, a family, i.e. a support system), not externally (by the price mechanism). And in this light, the Directors Company was nothing but a perversion of American Zoetrope.

Grounding the Corporation

For the moment, and for a strategic reason, we will bypass an important phase of Coppola's career—following his 1974 coup d'Oscar, when both *The Conversation* and *The Godfather, Part II* received Best Picture nominations and the latter film won it, Coppola began an embattled decade-plus in the industry during which his corporate innovations, while in some respect laying the bedrock for New Hollywood, would make him persona non grata in the industry. His excesses of this period, *Apocalypse Now* (1979) and *One from the Heart* (1982), and the public spin given them, left Coppola a director-for-hire in the years 1983–87. Our focus now will turn, instead, to the film narrative culminating this period, *Tucker,* a work that counts as the last exegesis (to date, anyway) that Coppola would dedicate to his business idea. If his work had hitherto derived a kind of utopian energy from believing that by his own intervention he might reshape the economy—might set the conditions, that is, for his own work—then it's easy to see *Tucker* as Coppola's concession statement that, in fact, business is not the domain of contending ideas. Business, rather, is the domain of contending interests, where the suppression of ideas is as likely as their realization.

Coppola's concession to this *realpolitik* outlook on labor is marked, poetically enough, by the inversion of his relations with George Lucas. Where once Coppola was Lucas's patron, as Lucas was brought around to the belief that his art need not be incompatible with Hollywood business, by the time of *Tucker* it was Lucas's turn to act as Coppola's patron. When Lucas split from Coppola, precipitated by and marking the end of Zoetrope, he formed his own company, Lucasfilm, which signals in its very name that the community orientation of Zoetrope had given way to more individualist enterprises. "Now we have each founded our own production houses," Lucas said. "Coppola Film and Lucasfilm."[155] He said this in September 1977, just after the release of *Star Wars*, the movie that would make Lucasfilm a massive success relative to the intermittent successes of Coppola's companies. In forming their own companies, Lucas and Coppola separated out their sensibilities, which had worked in combined force for Zoetrope. "Francis spends every day jumping off a cliff and hoping he's going to land okay," Lucas said, but "my main interest is security." Though he would claim they shared a goal—"We want to make movies and be free from the yoke of the studios"—he did not see the project of redefining business practices in the name of such freedom as a happy one. When asked, "Are you having fun being head of Lucasfilms?" Lucas answered decisively: "No. I don't want to be a businessman."[156] He considered himself "more of a technician," or, as though part of a craft economy, an "artisan-cameraman."[157] And if it was "great" when he and Coppola "were together," because their differences "complemented each other," by the 1980s it was also an irretrievable part of the past.[158] By then, Coppola, having worked for-hire on *Peggy Sue Got Married* (1986) and *Gardens of Stone* (1987), required Lucas's clout to regain his autonomy, in some small measure, and get financing for his own project, *Tucker.* He felt humbled, he claimed, in asking Lucas for support. "I wanted to do something with George," Coppola said, "but I didn't know if he wanted to do something with me."[159]

The adjusted power differential between Coppola and Lucas takes expression in *Tucker* as an unequal partnership between form and content. While critics disparaged the movie for this reason, and audiences were nonplussed in kind, this nonetheless makes it one of the more vexed and interesting documents of New Hollywood self-knowing. This owes chiefly to Coppola and Lucas holding such radically different views on what gives the corporation its proper grounding. In my earlier discussion of Lucas's cathexis on underground and experimental art (despite his having produced very little of it) as the counterpart to his phobia of mainstream and routinized commerce (despite his having produced great amounts of it), it should be clear that Lucas did not believe that art should acknowledge in its very form the social demands placed upon it, not insofar as these demands are overwhelmingly those of the marketplace. He believed, rather, in the denial of such demands; this is why he doesn't enjoy being and doesn't "want to be a businessman," because when in that mode he cannot be an artist. The split, for Lucas, is so absolute that his art must repress present-day commerce in favor of nostalgic pasts (the "artisan-cameraman") or far-flung futures (Star Wars, here, as the daydreaming done during Lucasfilm board meetings). His ex-wife Marcia, Lucas relayed, said that he "either live[s] in the past or in the future, never in the present."[160] This is one way of saying that he did not live—at least not in good faith—in the moment of the corporation's hegemony.

This is why Lucas wished for Coppola to reconceive *Tucker* in the mode of Frank Capra. As noted earlier, Coppola had first conceived *Tucker* in rather more epic terms, drawing into its narration the lives of historical personages such as Thomas Edison and Andrew Carnegie, but presenting this narrative in musical form, replete with Brechtian devices. "Instead of a philosophical inquiry," Robert Lindsey says, as Coppola might have had it, Lucas preferred, in his own words, "an uplifting experience that showed some of the problems in corporate America."[161] Lucas, in short, gave an odd prescription for both an exposé and a feel-good movie, two kinds of story that might not fit cheek by jowl; and for him it would seem that Capra—and what Jon Lewis calls his "peculiar populism"—was a kind of philosopher's stone that could turn the former story into the latter, that would convert the highly mediated environment of the corporation into an individualized setting of immediate action.[162] And perhaps Capra had this value. The content of the Tucker story—"an indomitable little man has a dream," as Lewis puts it, "of defying an indomitable big system"—sounds enough like *Mr. Deeds Goes to Town* (1936) and *Mr. Smith Goes to Washington* (1939).[163] But Capra told these tales in the interwar years, and only *It's a Wonderful Life* (1946) played for postwar audiences (whom Capra had kept primed for such stories, it's worth noting, with his *Why We Fight* films). In Jack Nerab's account in *The Hollywood Reporter*, Coppola at one point had even tried recruiting Capra himself for Tucker's story, but Capra turned it down because the story is not, in fact, one of individual triumph. However reliable this account of Coppola approaching Capra, it is indeed the case that when developing the script, Coppola and Lucas hired Arnold Schulman, who had written one of Capra's last films, *A Hole in the Head* (1959).

The point to be made is that telling a Capra tale after its historical moment had lapsed—after the form assumed by such tales stopped resonating—would, Coppola understood, leave the content inert, a message hanging in midair. Coppola took the real aesthetic problem to be a historical reckoning with the content's formal calcification; a problem, he believed, that would require an attack on form itself. This led critics to miss the point, as we'll see, and complain that *Tucker* is no more than an exercise in style. But the critical force of *Tucker* depends on our taking into account the corporate populism that licensed a Reagan-era modification in what we might call the deep structure of the corporation whose yield would be a privileging of its signifying practices over its labor practices. In short, what this meant in the Coppola-Lucas collaboration is that Coppola's hope of orienting the corporation around satisfying labor had been superseded by Lucas's compromise that the corporation might give labor some berth in relation to its satisfaction of the market. Corporate form, in itself, would offer no shield against market forces but rather, in the form of the bottom line, would be led entirely by them.

The most powerful account for how this played out in Hollywood is Justin Wyatt's study *High Concept: Movies and Marketing in Hollywood*, which explains the industrial restructuration known as New

Hollywood as the effect of marketing strategies reaching down into the very planning of film production. Steven Spielberg is the director most intimately associated with "high concept," as he was known for his "penchant for deliberating upon marketing schemes in advance of principal photography."[164] And it was, of course, with Spielberg that Lucas enjoyed his most fructifying collaboration after Coppola. So when Coppola came to collaborate with Lucas once more, it was in the context of the overturning of American Zoetrope's credo of utopian labor spaces. Granted, in Lucasfilm was preserved something of Zoetrope's inviolable regard for creative labor. Indeed, the president of Lucasfilm, Gordon Radley, says of the firm, "I don't know another company like this one" because Lucas is not "motivated out of a desire to make money" but rather to follow his vision.[165] However, now his firm protects not film labor writ large but instead only its specialized sector of tech workers. The total media enterprise must be profitable if the creative labors of one small branch are to be free and untrammeled. This, anyway, seemed to be the philosophy behind Lucas's business activity.

Even if this dismayed Coppola—his utopianism, after all, was more grand-scale—he understood it to be the new order of Hollywood business. His only recent success, *Peggy Sue Got Married* in 1986, was phoned in. "If that's what they want from me," Coppola fretted, "I'll give it to them."[166] If Coppola seemed to accept this business ethos, it would only be prelude to him making a retreat similar to Lucas's into more sectarian forms of autonomy. He claimed that *Tucker* would be "his final Hollywood movie" in an interview with Robert Lindsey for a *New York Times Magazine* story. "Two weeks from now," he said, "I'll be done here. I'll be free to do what I want. I'll be able to focus on things I want to do, not what other people want."[167] And, indeed, the domination of his labor by "what other people want" were the terms on which he made *Tucker*. He assented to Lucas's idea for the movie because he "knew George has a marketing sense for what the people might want." And what Lucas wanted, Coppola explained, was "to candy-apple it up a bit, make it like a Disney film."[168] In *Tucker* Coppola would make this movie in the only way he could understand it: as a disillusioned account of the illegitimate grounding of the corporation in a commitment to signifying practices that *told* people what they wanted rather than to labor practices that *let* people *do* what they wanted.

The real feat of *Tucker*, finally, is a deformation of content. The critic Stuart Klawans claims that the movie "poses a problem of imitative form."[169] The movie's form, that is, imitates advertising—namely, a Tucker industrial film. "It begins not as a 1988 Paramount Pictures megaproduction," Klawans explains, "but as a 1948 promotional piece for the Tucker Corporation, complete with bad color and kitschy music." But it does not stop. "When Coppola cuts away from this frame to begin the story proper," Klawans continues, "he has the nerve to be *more* hokey than the publicity film."[170] The movie never lets us escape from marketing language, verbal or visual, and hence never gives us any distance on its problem: this is not a movie about marketing cant, with movies an art form and advertising a hoax, but a movie about art's complicity with, and its perfecting of, advertising hoaxes. This is pop art; this is Hollywood postmodernism. The movie begins with a series of corporate logos, first the Paramount mountain, then a gold-plated Lucasfilm, and then the Tucker hood ornament. These logos mirror each other in an infinite regress that J. D. Connor says neoclassical Hollywood movies anxiously perform to stabilize their brand. In a kind of "logo bleed," as Connor dubs it, the logo detaches from its title card and merges into the very diegesis of the movie.[171] Here, however, the two authorizing brands, Paramount and Lucasfilm, pass into their authorized fiction, the Tucker Corporation, which was once as "real-world" as the Paramount and Lucasfilm brands that have authorized its necessarily fictionalized reappearance. What is fictionalized, that is, and what has been authorized to be so by Paramount and Lucasfilm, is that this movie is a form of public relations between its firms and their audience. This must pass for fiction, though Coppola's movie threatens its status throughout.

Even as the promotion begins, even as its stock sales voice crows about the Tucker car, "Pretty, isn't it?" over an image track of the car weaving through picturesque golden hills, the voice checks itself, as if an admission that the selling can't begin straightaway: "Mr. Tucker's car has everything—pop-out safety windows, rear motor. . . . Oh, but I'm getting ahead of my story." It then cuts to a photo album with the Tucker hood ornament embossed on its front, as though Tucker's childhood images have been retroactively shot through with the corporation's brand. As the Tucker film (the promotional film, that is, within Paramount and

Lucasfilm's promotional film) rolls on, we're told that Preston Tucker "never lost sight of his dream, which was to design and manufacture the finest automobile ever made." And as the words "design" and "manufacture" sound, we see in the frame two different forms of text, one diegetic and another nondiegetic. In an image of Preston Tucker and his wife, we see behind them a banner that reads "Automobile Manufacturers Exposition." This is the diegesis, as we're accustomed to understanding it. Over the same image, a credit for *Tucker* (Coppola's movie) reads "Sound Designer" and underneath, "Richard Beggs." The image and sound track have been coordinated, in short, so that the salesman's voiceover will read the words "design and manufacture" as we read these very words within the frame, once in the diegesis and once outside it. While we think of car manufacture, then, we necessarily think of sound design as a phase of film production.

The design of the movie bares itself, and it will bare itself again and again. To take only one instance of the movie's ostentatious design, it makes a point of staging all phone calls so that the people on opposite ends of the line are in the same space, with only thin illusionistic effects to suggest that they speak to each other from two distant spaces. Design is so much the essence of the movie that it's raised to the level of hyperdesign. For some critics, such as Terrence Rafferty, this is its problem. "Both people and objects seem overbearingly *designed*," Rafferty complains, "so that everything has a single, programmed significance and nothing is accidental."[172] No scene bears out Rafferty's criticism better than Abe Karatz's (Martin Landau) early visit to the Tucker household to discuss venture capital for Preston's idea. While Preston asks Abe whether Wall Street can "float stock issues" for an idea so revolutionary—when what's being revolted against is the Big Three trust—the Tucker kids are in the next room playing the board game Monopoly. The chosen child's game is, proof positive, the work of overall design.

This love of design transports us at once into the past and the future. On the one hand, there is the nostalgic design of the period piece being staged for us, everything in 1940s style. Here we perhaps make contact not with Capra's time, but with Capra's images of that time. On the other hand, there is the futuristic design of the Tucker car, its rocketship likeness, being staged for the characters in the diegesis. When Preston

Tucker unveils drawings of his car, his brother-in-law asks, "Who are we gonna sell 'em to, Buck Rogers?" It's easy to hear this as a reference to Lucas himself, who claims to have loved the Buck Rogers serials (and other old sci-fi serials) and to have based the formal design of the *Star Wars* movies on them. It's a futurism inscribed in a remembered past, a most complicated mediation, that is, of the present. And in this light we can see Tucker's drawings of his car as something like storyboards for the *Star Wars* movies, filled as they are with vehicles of the future. And, of course, this subject—automobiles—unites Coppola and Lucas, the two of them being owners of some of the only extant Tucker 48s, but in this moment the automobile joins their interest in a very complicated mediation of the present-day mode of production and the fetishized product designs it supports.

The puffed-up formalism of *Tucker* registers a malfunction in the mode of production that is always hidden by a most artful deflection of our interest, from the *thing* to the *imagined* thing. *Tucker*, crucially, is about the act of selling in the absence of a product. While Tucker had imagined innovations in a product, he was forced to advertise the image because he never had the capital to realize it as a product. The crux of the narrative is when Tucker, at a soda shop with his family, sees that a man is convinced that some advertised prefabricated housing is of high quality simply because a magazine tells him it is. "Have you seen one of these houses? How do you know they're any good?" Tucker asks him, adding, "They're not even built yet." "So what?" the man responds. "It says so in the magazine!" As Coppola remarks of the film's form, "We wanted the movie, in a way, to look like 1940s advertising art." He wanted "the look and feel" of the "new advertising phenomenon" in the moment, he says, that "color advertising started to appear in the magazines, giving people a taste of what the new product and the new period of postwar American preeminence" would bring.[173] The moment of Tucker's epiphany, in other words, is sparked by the magazine format. Coppola's act is hence what Jay David Bolter and Richard Grusin call "remediation," an act in which one medium tries to internalize for itself and transcend the properties of another medium.[174]

Coppola's remediation, though, is an interrogation not of the powers reposed in any given medium, and certainly not of the historical moment of magazine glossy advertising; it is, rather, an interrogation of the power that reaches across media platforms and merges cross-media messages into something charismatically transmedial. It is an interrogation of Coppola's historical moment of media industry conglomeration. Lucas, from some perspectives, was seen as having an answer to media-market fragmentation. Because he could exploit "ancillary" markets and "merchandising tie-ins," Jon Lewis says, he brought to the industry's attention a model of "pre-selling films as multi-industry products."[175] But the movie seems to critique this—the turn to Coppola Film and Lucasfilm—as the cynical application of auteurism. When the name floats free of the medium to sponsor come-what-may—when in the movie Tucker is told, "We're not just selling cars, we're selling you"—this obviously threatens to sever naming power from material reality. And the movie, of course, delivers us this premonitory warning: the Tucker name sits atop a factory that produces nothing, and is the title of a movie that rejects its own content. In short, Terrence Rafferty gives a perspicuous account of the movie when he writes that its "complexities" lie in the "relationship between the movie's content and the form that the director has imposed on it," and this relationship, misaligned as it is, protects us "from coming into contact with anything real." Rafferty, however, deploys this as criticism of the movie when it is nothing more than a description of its project.[176]

Preston Tucker learns the value
of advertising language.

Vocal Apparitions and Corporate Personhood:
Apocalypse Now, The Godfather, Part III, and *Tetro*

We can now return to the period of Coppola's professional undoing, from *Apocalypse Now* to *One from the Heart,* in light of the corporate failure that *Tucker* documents. My gambit is that we can only understand *Apocalypse Now*—an aesthetic fever dream—if we consider it in relation to the trajectory of Coppola's business idea, American Zoetrope. My point, put another way, is that we will only understand Coppola's unfolding aesthetic if we map it onto his theorizing of the firm as it is expressed, piece by piece, in his business enterprises. One plank in his aesthetic was this notion that representation, conventionally understood, should be short-circuited, such that a movie could not remain a consumable artifact without reference to its site of production. The two sites, I have argued, were reckoned together in Coppola's work. This can be recognized, at times, as Brechtian method, wherein a main goal is the audience's forced awareness that what they are consuming has been, and is being, made. Miriam Hansen remarks that the devices in *Apocalypse Now* create "Brechtian distanciation" so we might understand that the war "is being produced as we are perceiving it."[177] But Hansen is canny, I think, when she goes on to qualify the effect as "dislocation," not "distanciation." The spectator is not ejected from and made "external" to the spectacle, she argues, but is "caught in the mechanism with which the film—like war, like history—is being made."[178] Hansen's insight is crucial, for it does not rely on figuration of the external and the internal, but rather on undivided figuration. The spectator has no escape, being at once included in the process and captivated by its effect. "The real phenomenon of being in that situation, being in the middle of that jungle, and dealing with all the unfriendly elements," Coppola has said, "was part of what the movie was about."[179] The makers, in short, could not help but make their production-side experience the audience's reception-side experience.

Hansen's insight can be taken to account for another plank in Coppola's aesthetic: namely, his credal formulation of opera as a unitary figure of just this kind. The purpose of what follows is to explain how opera might be understood as a form of irreducible figuration, privileged by Coppola because it could not be broken into parts and still remain itself.

Further still, my purpose is to show that *Apocalypse Now* is precisely the moment in Coppola's career when doubt is introduced into opera's power of wholeness. It is still a high modernist movie, however, not the postmodernist movie that, say, *One from the Heart* so surely is. That, I argue, owes to *Apocalypse Now* being a record of Coppola's struggle to shore up this unitary figure despite its functional impossibility. After it, Coppola's cinema will lapse—as will his belief that business can have right orientation—into variants of the postmodern cynicism we find in *Tucker*. When he tries to reconstitute it, as he will, his cinema becomes consecrated not to opera as an active principle but as one irretrievably lost. Once we grant this, *The Godfather, Part III* and *Tetro* become fully intelligible, not only in their appearance as "fallen" versions of the original *Godfather* (*Tetro*, I argue, is the illegitimate sequel to the original, every bit as much as the eponymous third installment is) but in their curious and nonstop internal divisions within, and consequent misrecognitions of, the "family."

Coppola was part of a generation of filmmakers that displayed an outspoken debt to opera. Luchino Visconti might count as a forebear rather than member of this generation, but his example—as he moved between cinema and opera, cultivating an aesthetic by crossing the media—is central to Coppola, Martin Scorsese, Werner Herzog, and Hans-Jürgen Syberberg. Michael Powell and Emeric Pressburger were an equal influence for Coppola, as will become clear in the analysis of *Tetro*. In discussing what it means for opera to influence cinema, I will draw on Michal Grover-Friedlander's book on the topic, perhaps most conspicuously her title, *Vocal Apparitions*, which asks that we consider the stability of relations in what she calls the "vocal-visual dyad." This term describes the structure of image ("audio-vision," for Michel Chion) peculiar to cinema and opera alike, though the two arts negotiate such structure in, as it were, different dimensions. In Coppola's cinema, it's worth remembering that opera's influence is rooted in family; his father, Carmine, was a musician of classical training (who later would contribute music to his son's movies). Francis grew up in a musical household, where family life and opera nested one in the other. "In our family life," his brother August has explained, there was a "belief in opera." "If you sat at the family dinner table," he claimed, "you would understand why opera was born. When one of us was singing an aria, the rest had to stop and listen."[180] And being a childhood mainstay, it's not unexpected that opera remained a point of reference throughout Coppola's adulthood. Indeed, once *The Godfather* established Coppola's Hollywood career, he chose to direct Gottfried von Einem's *Visit of the Old Lady* for the San Francisco Opera.[181]

Though this registers as his only professional endeavor in opera, he often used the art as a mediating term in social situations. In Cuba, for instance, he recalls that though his tour group was first greeted with some suspicion by Captain Lindsay (a comrade, Coppola reports, of Fidel's in the Sierra Maestra), by the end of the first night he was drinking daiquiris with him and singing songs from the famous Cuban opera, *Cecilia Valdés*, a work that Coppola had gotten to know with his father. In another anecdote, Eleanor Coppola notes that while *Apocalypse Now* was in production in the Philippines, she and Francis sheltered members of the crew from a heavy storm in their rented home while Francis blasted *La Bohème* "full volume" on their phonograph.[182] Against the fragility of the social world, that is, Coppola sets the opera's logic of coherence. Because as a logic it has been historically overcome—the cinema having a centrality in twentieth-century culture that opera does not is a kind of proof for this—Coppola's cinema is constitutively exposed to incoherence.

My purpose is not to theorize intermedial relations between cinema and opera, nor even to account for the broad relevance that opera had for Coppola's generation. I find it suggestive, of course, that it was especially relevant for German, Italian, and Italian-American filmmakers, not simply because two main traditions of opera are German and Italian, expressed in an ultimate contrast between the barked Sprechgesang and the legato Bel Canto. But just as suggestive is what I take to be a homology between opera and the corporation in intellectual histories in which the German imagination conspicuously marked itself off from the Italian. These suggestive facts give a deep background for my purpose, which is to show how opera—and the history of ideas it encodes in its German and Italian traditions—gave compass for Coppola, since he was interested, as few have been, in the principles of aesthetic form and corporate form in equal measure.

Why these forms should overlap at all, when intuition tells us that art and business exist in discrete zones, is best illustrated in their common effort to solve a core problem of modernity: how it is that communities are organized and subjects integrated into them in the absence of transcendent values? An irresolvable question, certainly, but opera nonetheless can be understood as an effort to answer it. In the form of opera, Ivan Nagel argues, we can find the crisis of authority that results from the passage from traditional society into modernity.[183] Once bound metaphysically to authority, personhood now consults itself for self-definition. Hence opera seria, Nagel says, "always unfolds between two estates," with the "menacing" one called "god or monarch" on one side, and "man as subordinate" on the other side.[184] The no-longer-natural relation between these "two estates" is the social problem that opera takes for its object. For Nagel, this finds its high expression in Mozart's opera in the effort "to circumscribe that place at which the sovereignty of the One is supplanted by the freedom of the individual."[185] Call it the work of modernity, maybe the work of democracy, it is here being carried out in an aesthetic key. And for this reason, many have found it appropriate that Orpheus is the first figure of opera, for as an emblem of self-expression, he is called upon to reconcile his subjective powers with the object world. He is the lyric poet whose music, to gain a social function, Joseph Kerman says, would have "to inflame . . . the most frigid of minds." This is the "ultimate step" from "the lyric to the dramatic," and opera makes it by recruiting Orpheus for its project.[186] How the individual voice, i.e. lyric, is integrated into a community of voices, i.e. drama, amounts to the architectonics of opera.

But for this Orpheus is an odd figure. In both Monteverdi and Gluck, Orpheus loses Euridice outwardly in exchange for his inner formation. Because Orpheus cannot finally shape the outside world, he will anneal his inside world against it—his subjectivity will be reinforced, that is, by canceling the object world. On the face of it, the source of the subject's unitary form seems to be lyrical inwardness, but it comes from without. This is the trick, so to speak, of modern subjectivity: its source, lying in society, must be concealed if it is to give unity—or its appearance, anyway—insofar as the predicate of society, *difference,* cannot be rational grounds for unity. It's an obstinate paradox, displayed throughout the intellectual history of modernity, but for my purpose the point is that opera has given this problem musical form. It is, Nagel argues, the paradigm for Mozart's opera, where the "act of autonomy" is "modeled on magic, not on instrumental reason"—the "individual can round his existence into a whole," and "absurdly enough," as Nagel says, if, in Goethe's words, "quite unexpected things from outside come to his aid."[187] We see this dependent relation between the free self and the sponsoring polity, too, at the heart of Georges Bizet's *Carmen,* when Don José is caught between the love given him by society, the orphan Micaëla, and the love he gives himself, the Gypsy Carmen, and on following Carmen's credo ("Libre elle est née et libre elle mourra" [Free she was born and free she will die]), he finds not his freedom but his doom. And we see in Richard Wagner's *Lohengrin,* too, this prohibition on the subject discovering its source of autonomy. In it, Elsa is granted freedom, and her community assents to it, so long as she does not inquire into the identity of her liberator. Once she does, the strange mechanics behind her autonomy are exposed: she was freed by Lohengrin, guard of the Holy Grail, the sacred blood of which is the transcendental guarantor of community oneness. This bond obtains—it is transcendentally inviolable—only insofar as no one asks about it. If proof is demanded, the bond is gone. If any backing is demanded of the autonomy society grants, that is, it quickly becomes clear that nothing lies behind society's order; what it grants is provisional, not some endowment from above but some loose pact made within. Hence when Don José sets out to encounter his freedom in its absolute form, as when Elsa needs to know her freedom beyond its tenuousness, there is nothing to find: the subject finds its center gone and its self-issued autonomy collapsed.

I choose Bizet and Wagner here because Nietzsche chose them as composers in whose aesthetic difference, it seemed, he could not help finding political implications. In argument with Wagner, Nietzsche said that Bizet better understood opera's power: "What is good is light."[188] What "light" refers to, here, is not content (serious/frivolous) but structure (inwardly sound/outwardly fortified). When making a distinction between the men, Nietzsche referred to regional climate—Bizet's "southern, brown, burnt sensibility" versus Wagner's "damp north"— as if to make their aesthetic beliefs reducible to national character.[189] Less a concern with climate than with politics, Nietzsche's point would be that Bizet's opera is vigorous for finding sufficiency intrinsic in the voice, whereas Wagner's opera is moldering for its needing some extrinsic resource to complete its effect. Wagner, Nietzsche finds, did not trust his medium. Wagner's claim that his music was not "mere music" revealed this, insofar as "no musician would say that."[190] It could never be music *merely*. Doubts that the medium can carry meaning in itself are of the same substance as doubts in the audience. Bizet's "music treats the listener as intelligent, as if himself a musician," while Wagner "treats us as if—he says something so often—till one despairs—till one believes it."[191] Because no medium can alone bear the meaning of the work, which is a disguised fear that no one audience member singly can inherit the meaning of the work, Wagner turned to construction of the Gesamtkunstwerk. The "total work of art," as it's known, concatenated the various arts—poetry, music, and dance originally—to form a site, as did Greek theater, in which "sociopolitical and cultural unity" would be fostered "among its spectators."[192] This is unity through massification, which is "gigantic," Nietzsche says, but not "beautiful." [193] It might overwhelm with what is "great, sublime, gigantic," but it fails to imagine the mutuality that Sartre would later state as the existential relation between art and audience, wherein the work appeals to "the freedom of other men so that, by the reciprocal implications of their demands, they may re-adapt the totality of being to man and may again enclose the universe within man."[194]

This debate over aesthetics sounds different when transposed into jurisprudence, but it bears on the same intellectual problem: namely, the means of figuring the unitary character in a body of people. The problem, in fact, called for solutions in aesthetics (opera), politics (the state), and business (the corporation) that, no matter their efficacy individually, mark the conceptual order of modernity. If Wagner bungled things, in Nietzsche's opinion, by requiring an "associate work," thatching together piece by piece the work of the separate arts, jurists would handle it differently in theorizing the corporation. The parts do not matter—this legal tradition says—to the entity created by way of them. This is the tradition that German jurists such as Ernst Zitelman were articulating against a Roman tradition of associative wholeness.[195] Opposing a view that a "corporation is merely an abbreviated way of writing the names of the several members," Zitelman held that there was a "corporate organism" possessing "a will" that "is for that reason a real person."[196] The corporation is not shorthand for an enumerative act that might go on ad infinitum; instead, it unites itself in its will, and here Zitelman's language ("emheitlichen Willen") recalls Schopenhauer's *Wille* for the good reason that he was born into a Schopenhauerian mid-nineteenth-century Germany. His and other German theories of the corporation, whose importation into common law would give its corporate theory a coherence otherwise lacking, derived from Schopenhauer's concept of will, as did Nietzsche's earliest thinking on music *qua* the "immediate language of the will."[197] Corporate personhood and operatic subjectivity may each be incoherent finally, but they are incoherent for reasons of common intellectual descent. They form a discourse on unity within a differentiated whole—unity-in-difference, in short—for which Wagner is one kind of emblem in the popular imagination.

That, anyway, is how Francis Ford Coppola would use Wagner in *Apocalypse Now*. In one of the movie's canonical scenes, Colonel Kilgore (Robert Duvall) orders that Wagner's "Ride of the Valkyries" accompany the air-cavalry helicopter strike. The image of this helicopter fleet rising over the horizon with the sun, a display calculated to "scare the hell out of the slopes," according to Kilgore, is the image par excellence of Wagnerian militarism. What I shall do here is consider Coppola's twofold uses of Wagner's opera. On the one hand, his movie deploys it as part of its effort to produce total milieux, and this ought to be read critically as the imperial project's need to impose artificial environments. Wagnerian pageantry always conceals nature in artifice, and its military application would simply be self-reproduction on the greatest scales. On the other hand, Coppola's movie continues to express an interest in the operatic themes outlined above, in particular questions of personhood in relation to a unitary polity. In this context we can assess *Apocalypse Now*'s choice to narrate the Vietnam conflict in terms of a U.S. military operation to "terminate" its own colonel ("But this time it was an American," Willard says, "and an officer"). Not only is Colonel Kurtz (Marlon Brando) no longer recognized as a citizen within the U.S. polity, but he seemingly forfeited this national personhood when he became a member—even the founder—of another polity in the Cambodian jungle. The question of his citizenship, or personhood more generally, holds interest in direct proportion to the crew members accompanying Captain Willard (Martin Sheen), who seem largely unmotivated by their nation's imperial project. This lack of motivation, I will argue, is a problem when contrasted with Kurtz's power to motivate. While matters of motivated belonging here concern the national polity, my point is to refer such representations to Coppola's business career to show that the national disintegration on display in Vietnam became a vehicle for Coppola's displaced meditation on his corporate failures.

Let's begin by paying closer attention to the "Ride of the Valkyries" scene. Two matters deserve attention: recording technology and surfing. The enabling term of the film's portable environments is technology. From the opening scene, the widescreen image of swaying palm trees is displayed pristinely, only so that it might be doctored and distorted. A helicopter passes, and the palm trees are now seen through the rippling surface of their fuel, and then the fleet leaves a dust of Agent Orange, and the trees are seen through its tint. The movie's very first image, that is, shows technology as the agent of environment transformation, suggesting that the "theater" of war here carries an aesthetic valence every bit as much as a military one. Miriam Hansen remarks, however, a preponderance of "devices of mechanical reproduction" among the technology.[198] This is the case. We first hear Kurtz's voice on reel-to-reel tape; Clean (Laurence Fishburne) listens to his mother's cassette tape on the boat; we even see Coppola himself cross the screen, Hansen notes, as "the man with the movie camera." This self-consciousness of technology, and recording technology in particular, is raised to ironic heights in the "Valkyries" scene—ironic because it remains unclear which side is the proper target of what Kilgore calls "psy war ops." Though he claims it scares the enemy, he claims too that his "boys love it." The latter claim seems more plausible, finally, than the former. Why, after all, would the villagers below be any more afraid of amplified Wagner than they were of the helicopter's payload of bombs? The psychological battle is more likely waged for the hearts and minds of the U.S. soldiers. That helicopters are rigged with a sound system great enough to be heard over their roar, though it may declare a technological asymmetry between the United States and Vietnam, is more a reminder of why the U.S. troops should fight in the first place. The true irony, then, is that the total spectacle of technology turns out to be less able to incentivize a soldier's commitment than is the rogue soldier, Colonel Kurtz.

What incentivizes the U.S. soldiers, and indeed motivates the air-cavalry strike, is surfing. The movie's "surrealist" character, as Coppola called it, emerges most powerfully in the scenes with Kilgore, though it later returns most primordially in the scenes of Kurtz's compound. The surrealism of it is that the soldiers carry out war operations *as though they were* leisure activities, and what allows them to confuse the two—to forget the violence of battle in the face of the pleasure of surfing—is that Kilgore is a good officer. Willard puts it in more begrudging terms: "He wasn't a bad officer." But he concedes that Kilgore "had that weird light around him" that let others know "he wasn't gonna get so much as a scratch here." Kilgore is a good officer in a sense conventional for the time, the same sense that would make him a good manager: he gets his men to tolerate their work by loving its rewards. This is the spirit of Fordism translated into battlefield morale. Kurtz, by contrast, has overcome the legerdemain implicit in this style of management and inspired a different order of motivation in his followers. He felt the need, as Greil Marcus puts it, "to be motivated by great feelings of love," and his was "a revolt against the ability of the U.S. government, the U.S. Army, to trivialize the life-and-death situation" and leave its soldiers "not motivated by great feelings."[199] They are motivated by surfing, by the weak illusion produced when leisure time masks the principle of necessity (expressed here, as Marcus says, as the "life-and-death situation"). "Charlie don't surf," Kilgore says, as a way of noting the differential regimes of leisure and necessity in Vietnam and America. "They choppered in the T-bones and beer and turned the LZ into a beach party," Willard observes. "The more they tried to make it just like home, the more they made everybody miss it." That Willard should remark the strained credibility that this portable milieu effects is the most serious critique the movie offers, for his is the central heart and mind at stake. He represents detached professional expertise, the form of labor most in need of conviction in America's postwar society, and it's clear that Willard is unconvinced by Kilgore's efforts but deeply compelled by Kurtz.

Here we ought to mark the moral suasion, or lack thereof, in technology, not simply because it seems to be the subject of the movie but because it had always been the upper hand that American Zoetrope thought it had on the Hollywood establishment. So Coppola had reasoned, anyway. It's the fallacy of this reasoning, and the doubt it cast on Coppola's business future, that makes *Apocalypse Now* interesting in so many perspectives. The movie is interesting, to wit, from the industrial perspective of New Hollywood practices; from the biographical perspective of all that Coppola had at stake, his personal property and his corporate prerogatives; and—as its "surrealism" attests—from the textual perspective of film aesthetics. And in this latter perspective, the movie gains multivalent interest because it thematizes its uncertainty about what technology's effects will be. At Cannes, Coppola said that the movie was not a representation of Vietnam but a reenactment of it. "We had access to too much money, too much equipment," and Coppola claimed that this caused them to "little by little" go insane.

"Too much equipment" is the obvious theme of the USO Playboy Bunny scene. As Willard and crew approach an army outpost, decked out as a makeshift USO stage, Clean calls the carnivalesque light riggings a "bizarre sight in the middle of this shit." On a river snaking through the jungle, they come upon fairground electrification, with wheels of light agleam and towering "lit phalluses," as Hansen puts it, ringing the stage.[200] Lance later comments, "This is better than Disneyland," which is the handiest model of a portable environment, one whose artifice is outspoken. The equipment, and the artificial environments, though, will not make the movie. (In *One from the Heart*, we might say that this is the lesson learned.) What will make the movie is charismatic performance, and this is thematized within the movie in Willard's acknowledgment of Kilgore's "weird light" and his fascination with Kurtz. Though Kilgore has great lines—"Napalm in the morning" ranks the twelfth greatest on AFI's list of all-time movie quotes—they required Robert Duvall's voice to bear them, because it has a plaintive catch in it, a kind of hoarseness assuring us of the humanity of his barked orders. Eleanor Coppola says that Duvall was "radiating energy" on the set, and "everyone could feel it."[201] He is a "good officer" for this reason, but the energy is lodged in, and is inseparable from, his personal presence. Willard feels it, but he knows that its charismatic power cannot extend into the space external to Kilgore. It is not technologically reproducible as an environmental surround. The put-on beach party doesn't convince his soldiers of home but reminds them of its absence.

This is why, I believe, Willard dwells so long on Kurtz in his mediated form, the tape-recorded voice and dossier reports. He is impressed that in mediated form some of Kurtz's charisma has communicated itself over distances. "I felt like I knew one or two things about Kurtz," Willard says, "that weren't in the dossier." Surely Willard is in part persuaded by tales that "this Montagnard army" of Kurtz's attend and "worship the man like a god," following his "every order, no matter how ridiculous." Kurtz's charisma, in other words, passes through his followers, whose obedience to him registers but cannot replicate whatever quality is intrinsic to him. Yet this narrative of obedient followers is one Willard has only heard, never experienced, and still he feels that he knows something about Kurtz that exceeds these narrative means. For this reason, the act that occupies Willard—an act I take to allegorize the movie's own aesthetic project—is the act of coordinating Kurtz's voice and image.

The movie signals this as its project in the scene at Nha Trang when Colonel Lucas (Harrison Ford) hands him a portrait and asks, "Captain, you've heard of Colonel Walter E. Kurtz?" He proceeds to play the recordings of Kurtz's voice intercepted from Cambodia. The voice, Lucas tells us, has been "verified" as Kurtz's, calling attention more to the instability than the certainty of its attribution. And when Lucas hands the photograph of Kurtz to Willard, he spills Kurtz's file on the floor, as though a gesture needed to conspicuously indicate that *constructing* Kurtz is their project. The voice is to be matched with the person, in this game, and General Corman takes the photograph and narrates it: "Walt Kurtz was one of the most outstanding officers this country's ever produced," he says, as if to give Willard a how-to demonstration. This project of designing an authoritative voice, Coppola would have us understand, is the project of cinema as well as the project of the corporation. If there is crisis reposed in "speech lacking the corporeal ground of a speaker's body," as Ivan Kreilkamp says of *Heart of Darkness,* then so too are there the basic potentialities of cinema and the corporation.[202] This, Coppola admits, was his earliest insight into recording technology. His father took him "to Studio 8H at NBC" and put him in the "glass box" to watch Toscanini, and there he had a knob to control the volume: "That just blew me away when I was a kid, when I realized that picture and sound were *not* connected!"[203]

Hence, an insight into cinema is being worked out in the Nha Trang scene, as Corman and Lucas both show the separateness of Kurtz's voice and image and suggest how one might connect them; but that the two men are named Corman and Lucas—after Coppola's first boss Roger Corman and Coppola's onetime corporate partner George Lucas—suggests that this exercise with Kurtz is meant to illustrate the principles of cinema and the corporation at once. Kurtz's charismatic voice, after all, has an uncanny power to organize purpose within a group. "These are his children," the photojournalist (Dennis Hopper) tells Willard. "You don't talk to the Colonel, you listen to him," he says, adding that as a reward for this obeisance, "the man's enlarged my mind." Kurtz has not enlarged his society, nor his circle of friends, but rather he has enlarged his mind to include those relations within it. He has "re-adapt[ed] the totality of being to man," in Sartre's words, such that man "may again enclose the universe" within himself. This is corporate unity, rather than its weak counterpart—membership—and the project assigned Willard of putting together the voice and image of Kurtz ("They think you've come to take him away," the photojournalist says, "and I hope that isn't true") is finally an experiment in whether Willard can assume Kurtz's charismatic voice. The experiment, that is, tests whether the body must be the ground for the voice. Kurtz, we learn, "is dying" because "he hates all this"—"this" being, we infer, the "pagan idolatry" of his body as origin of group purpose—but "the man really likes you," the photo-journalist tells Willard, and "he's got something in mind for you" because "you're still alive." All of this, from Dennis Hopper, plays as an abstract rant of the drug-addled. "You can't go out into space, you know," he later rants, "with fractions—what are you gonna land on, one-quarter, three-eighths?" Once we recognize, though, that our reference point is the primordial unity between body and voice, Hopper's rant is fully intelligible. "You're gonna help him," he tells Willard, because "he dies" when "it dies," and hence the project Kurtz has "in mind" is for Willard to assume the voice that, in a primordial outlook, must attach to the body but, in a modern outlook, must be capable of decoupling from it. Fractions versus wholes, as Hopper puts it, are absolutely pressing matters if one is to distinguish associated members from unified groups.

The genius of the group—which is what Kurtz emblematizes—must survive its own embodiment. This is a curious thought experiment to enact in the middle of a story about the Vietnam War, but its logic becomes inescapable when we recognize two things. First, Coppola had understood that the Fordist habit of separating production and consumption, labor and leisure, is most obviously flawed when seen in the context of the Vietnam War. The surfing episode suggests that stateside leisure is bought in the coin of exported misery. Hence a new corporate model, whether commercial or political, is required. But second, after his run of corporate failure, from American Zoetrope to the Director's Company, Coppola had serious doubts that the modern solution could withstand the abrasion of primordial beliefs—that, in short, the genius of the group *could* survive its embodiment. His moment of doubt, it turns out, would become infamous, not because making *Apocalypse Now* drew forth his megalomania but because he documented it in a memo to his staff at American Zoetrope.

In November 1977, *Esquire* published a memo intended only for Coppola's associates, which, by "a bureaucratic slipup," made its way to the magazine editors. An outline of "the nature of my Company," it is a unique document for the reason that it reverses the principles of American Zoetrope absolutely but seems to lack conviction in doing so. "This company," he declares, "will be known as AMERICAN ZOE-TROPE and, purely and simply, it is *me and my work.*"[204] As if needing to overstate the embodied nature of his company, he writes, "Wherever I am will be considered the headquarters for the company, whether in the United States or somewhere else in the world."[205] He here invokes, for himself, the same charismatic singularity that lets Kurtz bind together his own polity, but in doing so Coppola can only justify it in atavistic terms. "You really are not employees of a company," he explains, but "instead, the staff of an artist."[206] He requires the terms of an artist's workshop, the great master in relation to his apprentices, as though this model held sway in settings other than a feudal economy. He goes so far as to dictate the forms of speech permitted his staff: "Please make your statements or questions as short, simple, and as easy to answer as possible."[207]

This business model, though, gives up the ghost of American Zoe-trope, and Coppola registers great anxiety about this. "In the past," he admits, "the nature of the company has been referred to as a 'family' or a club or a hangout." And this—from the time of visiting Mogens Skot-Hansen's Lanterna studio, where "they would all have lunch together in the garden," to the "cookouts in the back of the sound trailer" on *The Rain People*—was precisely what Coppola had wanted. He concedes the point. "I know in the past that I have encouraged this," he writes, "but, simply, I have changed and I no longer see this as a viable way of working." The change he names sounds more like the breaking of his spirit—or the performance of a broken spirit for the sake of encircling creditors, as the case might be, when he notes how "very important" it is that he "dispel the seven-year ambience of a hippy hangout." If Zoetrope cannot stay true to its original spirit, then its failure, Coppola seems to believe, attests to the triumph of the model it had meant to overthrow. He advises his employees, accordingly, to think of Zoetrope as "your place of business," and this implies that people should "dress and behave as they would for any other company."[208] They are no more than organization men working at another's behest. And yet what belies his advocacy of status quo business practices is that, finally, he still wants "relaxed and warm" relationships in the workplace. He does not want anyone to feel "like an automaton employee in an office job." And while he is "planning to help out talented newcomers in some viable and practical way," this help will come "not through Zoetrope"—which has been reduced to a "one-client studio," its work dedicated to "my films and my theater projects solely"—but through some undisclosed agency.[209] That is to say, somehow the corporation, which once he had imagined as the agency for internalizing and hence equalizing relations, had failed its charge. His company was now radically collapsed into himself, and, if we take this memo at its word, the only mode for relating to others in the future was not as family ("My family," as he now restricts it, "consists of my wife and three children") but as externalities, on a playing field governed by contracts between economic individuals which Ronald Coase deems prior to the firm.[210]

There is reason not to take the memo as the last word, especially when Coppola's next enterprise would be a seeming recommitment to Zoetrope but now on Hollywood scales. My point here is to look ahead not in the direction of corporate endeavors but in the direction of opera aesthetics. In *Apocalypse Now*, Wagner is the music chosen for the enhancement of military theater because Wagner is the composer to deny that "all opera is Orpheus," as Theodor W. Adorno put it—to deny opera, in effect, its great power of testing the limits of voice, hopeful that no meaninglessness lay beyond it; Wagner's denial, as Grover-Friedlander explains, "threatened the future of opera as such."[211] Wagner's "attempt at totalization," she says, "expresses itself as musical saturation, which overwhelms song." Hence Coppola uses Wagner, unlike the Verdi used in *The Godfather*, to mark the end "of the old vision of opera," which is also the end of one fantasy of personhood.[212] The personhood at stake is modernist, we should say, in that it believes that an upshot of the post-metaphysical age can be mutual understanding (the voice *qua* subjectivity) rather than mutual destruction (aesthetic pageantry *qua* military display). If the personhood facing extinction had been elaborated in various domains—the philosophical, for instance, or the political—for Coppola, its key failure is in the most practical domain of a modern economy: the corporation. What we see in *Apocalypse Now* is Coppola's concern with failed models of personhood expressed as a concern with opera aesthetics, specifically as they are misapplied on the notion that operatic grandeur comes from the production of totalized environments, such as the bedecked Bayreuth, when in fact it comes from the voice, which is unitary when it compels in its audience conviction in its medium.

Mechanized Family

Briefly, I want to consider later instances of opera in Coppola's cinema, to show both what they say about his theory of cinema and how his view on opera evolved. For this, his most compelling movies are *The Godfather, Part III* and *Tetro*. The final installment of the *Godfather* series has been variously assessed, not always as "compelling," with many critics considering it a steep drop in quality from the previous movies. Coppola defends against this, in some respects, by calling it an epilogue to the series rather than a full-fledged entry. But whatever its overall merits, it is at the very least a rigorous coming to terms with opera and its influence on Coppola's cinema, his career, and the role of the franchise within it. Though the first *Godfather* had Verdi's music in it, and *Apocalypse Now* so boldly featured Wagner, the final *Godfather* is Coppola's first movie to make an explicit place for opera in the story, using an opera house as a set, opera singing as a career choice, and so on.

The Godfather, Part III is dedicated to opera as a kind of open declaration that the *Godfather* franchise had been all along. In it, Michael Corleone's son, Anthony (Franc D'Ambrosio), chooses to become an opera singer rather than study law and become the family's consiglieri. "I will always be your son," Anthony tells his father, "but I will never have anything to do with your business." This scene is not much more than a retread of the dialogue between Michael and his father in the original movie, where Vito tells Michael that he had wanted him to be

"Senator Corleone, Governor Corleone." The father wants legitimacy, the son refuses it—or anyway, he refuses legitimacy *in this form.* "I think that was a shameful ceremony," Kay says of Michael's criminal empire being "disguised" by his church in return for his philanthropic support. Here she only reminds him of what he knew already when his father sought legitimacy in this form, and what his son Anthony still actively knows: this is the legitimacy given to only "another *pezzonovante.*"

But if this, by now, is but a stock scene in the franchise, the alteration in the framework accommodating it is entirely novel. The Corleones retain their monopoly on power, as they had in each previous movie, but what they now do that they had not in the past is gain sanction for it through cultural rather than political means. The coercive force of power had never held interest in these movies to the degree that the persuasive force of power did. Michael has been a study in tragedy because he misunderstood the source of his father's power, believing that it derived from the *force* of decisive action, when in truth it derived from the *show* of decisive action. Vito held a family together through the consent of its members, whereas Michael presided over a family's slow disintegration, as he tried coercing its togetherness. By the final *Godfather* episode, we understand why the two had opposite effects: Vito showed his family that he decisively acted for their sake, with violence only incidental to this action's efficacy, but Michael had violently insisted on their obedience, all the while explaining to them that his violent insistence was for their sake. Kay sees the difference. "Reason backed up by murder," she tells Michael, has done nothing to convince anyone that he "spent [his] life protecting [his] son . . . protecting [his] family," a conviction that Vito never had to do anything to solicit. The family's loyalty, such that any remains—and Sonny's illegitimate son, Vincent (Andy Garcia), remains utterly loyal, it should be said, and so too do Michael's children, Mary (Sofia Coppola) and Anthony—looks like little more than a biological function: "I will always be your son," as Anthony says.

In this regard, the final *Godfather* is a matter of figuring out what went wrong. Michael figures this out, somewhat reluctantly, by returning the family to the opera. Coppola depicts the modest restoration of Corleone authority on precisely the model that Slavoj Žižek explains operatic personhood. "The first rudimentary form of subjectivity," Žižek claims, "is this voice of the subject beseeching the Master to suspend, for a brief moment, his own Law."[213] Such a scene is enacted to the letter in the opening scenes of the movie. Kay has come to Michael's ceremony on Anthony's behalf, so that he might get Michael's blessing to quit law school and pursue opera singing. The Master, Michael, declines at first, but then, when it seems that mercy will be withheld, he grants Anthony the autonomy he needs "to go free and have his own life." There is, in this, the Hegelian logic of Master and Servant, as Žižek observes there must be in opera, disclosed in the fact that Michael now sees what his work is and understands it from a perspective below, one allowed those who worked under him (and were near rebelling against him), and it is precisely this perspective that could redeem him, if anything could. Letting his son sing opera, Michael restores his wholeness as sovereign and inaugurates "a new period of harmony" in the family's life.

When Anthony has sung the tenor in *Cavalleria Rusticana* to the acclaim of a Sicilian audience, Michael tell his sister, Connie, "When they hear the name Corleone, they're gonna think of a voice." Here Michael is hailing the cultural legitimation of his family empire by eliding the fact that the substance of their legitimacy comes from purchasing a corporation, International Immobiliare, with the fact that the style of their legitimacy is sealed in the operatic voice. Their wealth is now legally protected by a corporation, but their authority is now culturally secured in the acclaim of their unitary purpose, the Corleone voice. Coppola is remarkably canny to show that the voice of the family, Anthony, on succeeding, is first greeted by the muscle of the family, Vincent. Anthony and Vincent embrace, figuring the interlocked legitimacy and illegitimacy of the family, and Vincent remarks of Anthony's peasant-soldier costume, "I like this outfit." The response: "I figured you would." The violent barbarism of the family, in short, benefits most from misrecognizing itself on stage as legitimate cultural expression. And in case we do not understand this to be the movie's clarion message, it has been demonstrated for us already: in an early scene, Vincent bites Joey Zasa's ear while embracing, and in a later opera scene, Vincent looks on, smiling, as Anthony repeats his action, in the role of Turiddu biting the ear of Alfio. And formally, we cannot fail to see that the movie's plotted actions—assassins placing Michael in their crosshairs, Vincent's henchmen performing assassinations of their own—are embedded in the opera's form. This was true of the *Godfather* movies all along, of course, but now it is made explicit.

The story of the family attaining corporate and operatic form all at once is still a tragedy, however, for the simple reason that Michael has understood the family's peculiar structure of personhood too late, and for the complicated reason that Coppola no longer believed corporate personhood to be anything more than a ruse, in practice, even if he still believed it to be liberatory in theory. On this count, I'd like to make a few speculative remarks about *The Godfather, Part III* as a kind of preamble discussion for *Tetro*, which I take to be Coppola's rewrite of the *Godfather* for his own purposes. Setting the final *Godfather* in 1979, while it makes good narrative sense, has as much symbolic as narrative value. The year marks the end of a historical period, on the one hand, a period of political economy that finds its symbolic closure in the election of Ronald Reagan and the rise of the conservative movement; on the other hand, it marks the release date of *Apocalypse Now* and the last good year of Coppola's career.

The diegesis of the *Godfather* trilogy covers an era of political economy, even if through a glass darkly. But the production years of the trilogy, 1972–89, cover an era of New Hollywood in which questions of ownership and authority were renegotiated. With this movie franchise, Coppola says, "there was the possibility of having a company that could one day evolve into a real major company and change the way we approach filmmaking."[214] No such thing happened, of course, and by 1989 Coppola was compelled to make a final *Godfather* installment simply to get out of debt. Jack Singer had been "demanding that Coppola repay the $3 million he had loaned him to help finance *One from the Heart*."[215] Not only did Coppola decide to take on the final *Godfather* because, by this point, no other project gave him the same level of bargaining power; he took it on, too, because he did not want to be displaced by another director. Paramount seemed ready to do the movie one way or another, and they had considered directors such as Martin Scorsese, Sidney Lumet, and even Michael Mann. "It's a little bit like hearing that your ex-girlfriend is going out with so-and-so," Coppola said of the situation. "You don't care. But you *do* care."[216] He made the movie his occasion to get out of debt and to sum up the career possibilities left to himself and his colleagues in New Hollywood. In the movie, Michael Corleone buys a "European conglomerate," a kind of fantasy relation between Coppola and what by then was the principal corporate structure in Hollywood industry. But also it uses the opera *Cavalleria Rusticana* to cross-reference the career of Scorsese, who had used the interlude from the opera in the opening scenes of *Raging Bull* (1980), and this cross-reference is made, I submit, because Scorsese, like Coppola, had spent the 1980s working for-hire in a New Hollywood increasingly uncongenial for their talents.

The final *Godfather* is at once a reckoning with New Hollywood—the "newness" of which marks, for Coppola, the squandered chance to fuse art and business—and a forecast of the ways in which good work might still get done within such arrangements. If in this possible future Michael owns the conglomerate, he seems to have set up an artistic wing (Anthony's voice) that will be financed by the family's brutal economy (Vincent's violence). The family, not a unit now but a set of parts, has folds within it where each part might fulfill itself irrespective of the others. This is an accurate enough foretelling of 1990s Hollywood, one in which Coppola would want no part, where independent production companies such as Good Machine and October Films were formed on their own but then drawn into the large conglomerates, and where, too, Coppola and Scorsese would reestablish their industry power on very different terms (the former from without, and the latter from within). What is most compelling in *The Godfather, Part III*, though, is the extent to which Coppola has used it to make an argument, in an aesthetic register, for why this foretold model can only fail. Its failure, in fact, is marked in opera's failure—Michael (and Coppola, as it were) will sacrifice a daughter to it. Mary leaves the opera house and is hit by a bullet intended for Michael. This—I suggest in some reflections to come on Sofia Coppola's career—has a very specific meaning in respect to Francis Ford Coppola's corporate aesthetics: Anthony is operatic personhood, the movie tells us, but Mary is pop-song individuality. The final expression is the father's anguish, which must be operatic anguish but can only reach us through cinema: Kay holds Mary's dead body on the grand staircase, and Michael kneels by himself nearby, his mouth gaping in a voiceless cry. As Michael's mouth widens, and as he throws his head back, we hear Mascagni's strings rise in a kind of melodic voice that we ought to hear as a substitute for Michael's own. His mouth is open, and

In a voiceless cry, Michael brings forth
his pain, too late.

drool runs down his chin in a string, as it does for opera singers as they produce inhuman sounds, or sounds anyway that are the upper limit of our humanity. The image of Michael waiting for his voice, as the score matches his movements as would the score in *Alexander Nevksy* (1938), is Coppola's audacious statement, nearly a valediction, on the cinema's exceptional powers for reordering the vocal-visual dyad. In this sense the *Godfather* trilogy is not the story of a man who must find his voice and authority but is a demonstration that this voice and authority floats free and therefore present themselves to various reordering. Cinema can do this, and so too can the corporation. This is why, I speculate, Coppola would need to conclude the story himself, so that another didn't miss the point.

But Coppola, as his subsequent career attests, was not content scoring points off Paramount by arrogating the last *Godfather* for his own state-of-the-industry meditation. To depict a flawed corporate structure, with sham family feeling at its center, was not enough to exhaust his Zoetrope ambitions. Instead, Coppola would use the 1990s to build a third incarnation of American Zoetrope; this time its orientation owed more to John Cassavetes than to the corporate utopians of the 1960s. More can be said, in another forum, of the change these different versions of American Zoetrope clock in Hollywood economic practices in particular and global political economy in general.[217] But for now we might risk a simplified history in the progression of American Zoetrope from utopian family firm (1969–72), to artistic soup-up of the Hollywood factory (1980–82), and finally to a boutique company whose years of operation are more ill-defined, split as the operation is between wine-making subsidies (dating to his 1975 purchase of the Niebaum vineyard); producing his children's movies, Sofia's notably (dating to her first feature, *The Virgin Suicides,* in 1999); and independently making his own small-scale movies (dating to the first movie of his "second career," *Youth without Youth,* in 2007). The problem with this model of American Zoetrope is that it finances movies, as did Cassavetes, not from their intrinsic value but from extrinsic sources. Cassavetes predicated his artistic vocation on a robbing-Peter-to-pay-Paul principle, taking income from whatever acting jobs so that he might direct movies that interested him; the problem is that the seeming vocation starts to look like avocation, as a day job might support one's weekend passion, the suggestion being—finally—that one cannot make a livelihood from what one loves.[218] "The great frustration of my career," Coppola admits, "is that nobody really wants me to do my own work."[219] This predicament, made axiomatic, is a negation of the original ethos of American Zoetrope. Yet it's roughly true to say that Zoetrope, such that it now exists, is the inverse of its founding business idea. Originally Zoetrope took money from within Hollywood industry, whether from Warner Bros. or from Coppola's own movie profits, and planned on using those resources against tendency. When Coppola made *Tetro,* by contrast, he did so from the profits of his outside enterprises, "wine, but also including cigars, a line of prepared foods, two restaurants, and three Central American resorts."[220] This is the synergy (in another idiom, "hedging") that became the watchword of the conglomerates. What synergizes his diverse products, Coppola explains, is himself: "My company, FFC Brands, sells my taste."[221] It is the final irony that he would need to make American Zoetrope a filmmaking arm in his larger conglomerate in order to make movies again in the age of conglomerated Hollywood.

It is therefore unsurprising that *Tetro,* the product of this generation Zoetrope, should be so equivocal a statement. Coppola was able to make the movie on his own terms, certainly, but Zoetrope, his critics said, had failed "to deliver on its grand plans." He conceded that, in early versions of Zoetrope, they "were in a cocoon," but still insisted that the studios, as they were, would disappear. "Art studios will replace them," Coppola predicted. "This is my dream."[222] My purpose is only to explain why this dream is still encoded in opera aesthetics, curious though they are, in *Tetro*. In part, the explanation is that because the *Godfather* trilogy was told in opera's idiom, *Tetro*, being an alternative telling of *The Godfather*, must take the form of opera as well. Larry Rohter remarked that *Tetro*, another "drama about an Italian immigrant family in conflict," ranges over "some of the same territory, albeit from a different direction," as did the *Godfather* trilogy.[223]

There are more details placing it in line with the *Godfather* trilogy than the mere subject of an Italian family in conflict. Bennie (Alden Ehrenreich) arrives at his brother Tetro's Buenos Aires apartment in a navy uniform, as Michael had arrived at the family home in marine fatigues. The joke, here, is that for Bennie the uniform is not a true navy uniform but an imitation worn by employees of Infinity Line cruise ships. Benne is "a waiter, sort of." And Vincent Gallo, playing Tetro, had in a sense already auditioned for a part in the *Godfather* movies, perhaps Fredo's, when he played Paul Leger in *Arizona Dream* (dir. Emir Kusturica, 1993). In it, he watches *The Godfather, Part II* and recites the famous lines exchanged between Michael and Fredo: "Fredo, you're nothing to me now. You're not a brother, you're not a friend. I don't want to know you or what you do." But it's Gallo's recitation of Fredo's lines that show the most uncanny resemblance. "Taking care of me? You're my kid brother and you take care of me," Gallo quotes in the tremolo that marks Fredo as the weak brother.

The dialogue can be applied to *Tetro*, the story of a man who renounces his family relations. "How come you say I'm your friend and not your brother?" Bennie will ask Tetro. This *Godfather* rewrite takes on interest, I contend, because the rivalry between brothers is set not against a backdrop of crime but of the arts. Tetro is a writer, and so is his brother, Bennie, and the story Tetro begins writing, but gives up, is the story of two brothers: "one brother, a prodigy in music, and the older brother, also a great musician." On hearing this, Bennie responds, "You're writing the story of our father?" The need to rewrite the father's story as one's own, it needs no heavy underlining, is what gives *The Godfather, Part II* its pathos. Michael cannot replicate his father's family success, because Michael lacks an element of personality that was inherited, we might infer, by his brother, Fredo. It's possible to imagine that what occludes the telling of Fredo's story, or anyway what denies Fredo's story narrative fulfillment, is that he is more an artist than a businessman. He is the more sensuous of the brothers, at any rate, his instinct for hedonism marked in the family's sending him to Las Vegas. Were *The Godfather* retold as a family of artists rather than a family of criminals, Fredo's sensibility would be the heart of the story. "A family needs as much fun as it can get," Tetro's wife tells Bennie.

Turning the gangsters into artists, swapping out the cunning of Michael or the violence of Sonny for the sensuousness of Fredo, moves the story one degree closer to Coppola's own. In his telling albeit negative review, Richard Corliss remarks that Coppola's "father Carmine was a flutist for the NBC Symphony Orchestra," and Carmine's brother Anton was, at first, "the more renowned" brother as the "composer of a violin concerto and the opera *Sacco and Vanzetti*"; *Tetro* therefore plays as Anton's belated comeuppance.[224] Critics of Coppola's late work, in short, were accustomed to finding personal material allegorically reworked. Jon Lewis catalogues some instances of this critical habit, notably Stuart Klawans's response that *Life without Zoe* (1989) "becomes explicable only if" you consider it an allegory for American Zoetrope.[225] The personal material is there, no doubt, as *Life without Zoe* begins by defining the Greek "zoe" as life, a kind of sly nod to the itinerary of his firm, and it too features a father who is a flutist. But as Walter Murch has remarked, "one of Francis's great strengths" has been to find "ways to get his films to tap into his own personal experiences."[226] He identified with the material of *The Godfather* by rendering corporate capital—and the structure of the Hollywood studio in particular—as a crime story. This was, one presumes, the only way to tell this story on the studio's dime. Now that his stories are told on his own dime, as it were, he has moved from allegory to biography. The critics who find this uncomfortable do so, it seems, because now the storytelling is too on-the-nose. Without mediation, Klawans finds "unanticipated perspectives of egomania."[227]

What is telling in Corliss's criticism of *Tetro* is his claim that "Coppola fans want him to recapture the dramatic coherence and operatic grandeur" of his first *Godfather* movies.[228] I will take the license to suggest that Corliss, and other critics too, are registering their own regret that American Zoetrope did not realize its original vision because "the dramatic coherence and operatic grandeur" were only the sublimated form of its business idea. The notion that a firm could be run like a family of artists, and that "a family needs as much fun as it can get"—though it now seems musty, like the sixties—is what animated Zoetrope and the films designed to realize it in an aesthetic foretaste of its material instantiation. In *Tetro*, though, notions of authority and ownership are shot through with cynicism that family is but a set of relations mechanically performed. We know this because the opera it cites, in roundabout fashion, is that containing Coppélius (also Coppola, in E. T. A. Hoffman's original stories), maker of "the dancing doll." Its citation of opera, though, is routed through cinema, namely *The Tales of Hoffman* (dir. Michael Powell and Emeric Pressburger, 1951). The opera Powell and Pressburger adapted was Jacques Offenbach's *Les contes d'Hoffmann* (1881), itself an adaptation of Hoffmann's stories. This delirious remediation is the counterpart of the plot's similar involutions in family structure, wherein Bennie finally understands that Tetro, whom he thought was his brother (a next-generation Fredo), is revealed to be his father. Further ancestry is given: the original Benjamin Tetrocini, the movie explains, came to Argentina in 1901; he became rich in the wholesale chicken business, "but he liked to sing, and he played mandolin." Businessman by day, artist by night. We recognize this as the Fordist ratio that it was the charge of Tetro's (and Michael Corleone's) generation to overturn. Benjamin Tetrocini died, his gravestone says, in 1968—the year before the post-Fordist firm, American Zoetrope, was born.

Critics who find the plot's biographical backdrop too on-the-nose might be surprised to see how heavily mediated it is. When Bennie (an updated Michael) learns that Tetro (an updated Fredo) is not his brother but his father, after all, it is from Coppola a revelation of what Michael had misrecognized in his father: he thought the Don's authority came from "reason backed up by murder," when in fact it derived more fundamentally from the sensuous vulnerability of Fredo. The Don easily held authority, that is, because he was more like Fredo than Michael. This clarifies the confession Michael makes to the cardinal in the final *Godfather,* "I killed my father's son," to be a confession of an allegorical kind. It is a confession that Coppola, in capitulating to Hollywood's terms—which are only the terms of capital, after all—had killed his business idea. He

The opera of Coppélia's automaton. |

might make movies again, but now he has cast himself as the rapacious patriarch of an intact hierarchy. The automaton, designed by Coppélia, performs life without life (*Life without Zoe*), which is fallen labor and fallen opera at once.

Zoetrope Postmodernism
and the Amazing Technicolor Family

There is an odd scene in *The Godfather, Part III* that might have been lifted from another aesthetic world and smuggled into what had been, for the life of the trilogy, a *Godfather* diegesis tightly ordered on opera's principles. In the movie's second half, signaled by the Corleone family's transplantation back to Sicily, we see a tableau shot of an Italian villa, two open windows with curtains billowing on the left and right sides. What jars, here, is the song issuing from the left-side open window, Elvis Costello's "Miracle Man." As noted, the movie uses Mascagni's *Cavalleria* to refer to Scorsese's *Raging Bull*, and in doing so marks New Hollywood developments in the years intervening between this final installment and Coppola's last *Godfather* movie in 1974. But the movie uses Elvis Costello, we might suppose, to mark the pop song's incursion against what had been the symphonic sensibility of the Old Hollywood score. The song makes sense in a kind of twofold chronology: since the last *Godfather* was made, Coppola's cinema had suffered an ongoing abrasion of its opera aesthetic, and through its tatters emerged the rather less-orderly logic of the Hollywood musical. Coppola had made a musical early on—*Finian's Rainbow*—but he had always described this as an "other-directed" decision. "One of his motives was to impress his father," he admitted; another was to gain traction within studio Hollywood.[229]

If in the opera Coppola found a principle of centripetal force, with family ethos drawing stray individuality into its coordinates, in the musical he found something else altogether, something like the opera's antithesis. There, individuals sing out, in isolation, while the society enfolding them disintegrates. This explains why *Tucker*, when first conceived in the mid 1970s upon the failure of American Zoetrope and the Directors Company, was to be a "Brechtian musical," with MGM's Freed-unit veterans Betty Comden and Adolph Green its songwriting team. *One from the Heart,* however, is the "musical" (scare quotes to be explained) that in any telling must be said to put to rout Coppola's opera aesthetic. After it, all is disunity: Zoetrope is shuttered, Coppola works as director-for-hire the next decades, and never again is operatic unity his object of naïve aspiration. Costello's pop song, though, suggests another chronology. Simply, the last *Godfather* was set in the late 1950s, and in between then and 1979, the pop song had become the key form of youth-culture self-expression. The Beatles converted Buddy Holly into high art, and Elvis Costello, trading on Buddy Holly's image for his 1977 debut album *My Aim Is True,* became a kind of metacommentary on the institutional status of pop music. Mary Corleone grew up against this historical backdrop, as did Sofia Coppola, the actress playing Mary. Sofia, let's remember, was widely panned for her turn as Mary, which is expected given that the *Godfather* movies had been a showcase for magisterial performances, consecrated, in some respect, to "the Method," which had favored emotional displays shaded with operatic sensibility. Casting Lee Strasberg as Hyman Roth attests to this. Sofia's flat affect, in this context, fell short of all the established values. Far from a casting misstep, though, Sofia gives Mary flat affect—the ground tone, as it were, of pop-song individuality—because this had in fact been the competing theme in Coppola's cinema since *One from the Heart* and here, in his last for-hire concession, it had gained the upper hand.

Sofia would be the future of American Zoetrope. What I want to show, in these final pages, is how this can be deduced from *One from the Heart* and then, in turn, how it is that Sofia's *The Virgin Suicides* and *Marie Antoinette* can illuminate the former movie. *One from the Heart* is notorious. This has nothing to do with the movie itself, which is a brilliant work despite its critical panning. It has everything to do with the movie being the occasion for Zoetrope's regrouped effort to change Hollywood, this time through technology (the ballyhooed "electronic cinema") rather than the ethos of group-work ("I've also got good relationships with and promises of films," Coppola had once said of American Zoetrope, "from some of the more talented young filmmakers around").[230] Coppola still outwardly stuck to the principle of the "repertory company"—"In the Hollywood of today, everybody's an independent contractor," he complained; "I can't work that way"—but inwardly his studio was designed to overturn Hollywood's labor practices by way of its technological organization.[231]

Rather than describe what Coppola called the "electronic cinema," and rather than give an account of his enterprise to install Zoetrope on the Hollywood General lot, which Jon Lewis has done in his definitive study, *Whom God Wishes to Destroy,* my purpose is to show how the "other Coppola" emerged in *One from the Heart*—the one David Denby bemoaned for his sacrificed realism—and how it is that Coppola found a new aesthetic register in that movie, which anticipated Sofia's filmmaking approach.[232] Denby's critique that Coppola gave up realism for "artifice" is interesting because it presumes that Coppola's realism, based on *verismo* opera, wasn't already highly artificial. But it was, of course, and I contend that Coppola's 1970s cinema (the *Godfather* movies, *The Conversation*) is understood in half-light if not assessed in terms of musical artifice. "Movies are like music," he told visitors to Zoetrope Studios, "and should be composed along the same line."[233] But between the *Godfather* movies and *One from the Heart,* the musical experience is of a qualitatively different order. In *The Godfather,* voice is tied to its choral supports, even if the aria seems to lift it into autonomous heights; in *One from the Heart*'s boozy torch songs, though, it is the self reflecting on the self, opening up a subject's inner spaces which seem to stretch forever. The self's longing for infinite realization, untrammeled by social limitations, is here the structure of the pop song. This is the story of *One from the Heart:* a couple that will never understand each other—will never, for that matter, accept *an other*—in any mood but disappointment. This happens through a form of musical. But the musical form has undergone a technological mutation. "There is and can be content in technology," Coppola said. "New tunes that we've never heard before, because they've never been possible."[234] In moving from the *Godfather* movies to *One from the Heart,* and from Lee Strasberg to Sofia Coppola, one might say that we make the historical passage from the concert-hall experience to the headphone experience. In the former, a voice reaches us across great distances, and the structure of performance remains auratic; in the latter, a voice is placed in our ear, and the performance space is collapsed within. These, anyway, seem roughly the correct metonyms for their technological regimes.

One way to begin is by determining how *One from the Heart* might be classified as a musical. Coppola had contacted Tom Waits to write songs for the movie, his idea being that the songs would create a parallel track for the couple's story. Unlike "an old fashioned musical," Coppola did not want the characters to sing songs but wanted them rather to have a song-version of their lives running parallel to the mundane lived-version of their lives.[235] There is, in this, a loose approximation of the Hollywood musical, insofar as there is a rupture in the narrative world. In *An American in Paris* (1951), for instance, Gene Kelly plays a struggling painter but a brilliantly successful dancer. However, his painting is his real-life occupation, while his dancing is his fantasy-life expression. We thrill at him in the latter capacity but pity him in the former. This is the operation at work in *One from the Heart,* and clearly Coppola was taking cues from studio Hollywood in various ways. He shot the movie on sound stages, and he did so in the Hollywood General studios that had formerly been used by Harold Lloyd. Gene Kelly, in fact, was Coppola's advisor on the movie, as was Michael Powell.[236]

But Coppola works the musical's discontinuity to different effect. There is no Gene Kelly, no hoofer-in-disguise whom we recognize— through his powerful legs and trim physique set off by pleated slacks and tight sweater—as truly glamorous. Instead, Coppola has cast rigorously nonglamorous actors, Frederic Forrest as Hank and Teri Garr as

Frannie, and given them dowdy wardrobe to match. The couple tells each other as much. "You were pretty appetizing," Hank tells Frannie, "but now. . . ." Frannie shoots back, "What about yourself? You used to have a pretty good build, you know." The glamour has been commuted offscreen, into the sphere of song, and into the lavishly art-designed sets. Watching *One from the Heart,* we no longer cathect on the subjects but on the object-world suffused in their fantasies. Coppola claims that he "wanted the scenery, the music, and the lighting, for example, to be *part* of the film," an aim quite distinct from the classical high-key accentuation of the Hollywood star.[237] This flattening of the difference between subject and object is consistent with Sofia's latter-day flat performance and with what Jameson has named a key feature of postmodernism, the "waning of affect."

We can already see this as an intensification of the logic of *Apocalypse Now,* with the attention to totalized environments now overriding the charismatic voices at their center. In a final show of feeble voice, in fact, Hank tells Frannie, "I didn't come here to fight with you. I came to sing to you." Hank then delivers the shabbiest rendition of "You Are My Sunshine" to Frannie in the airport terminal; the only thing about it that touches Frannie ("That was nice," she says) is how inadequate his voice is for this stage. The stage, an unlikely reconstruction of Las Vegas on Hollywood sound stages, is beautiful. In this scene, Hank is awash in pale green light, and as he walks away in disappointment, Vittorio Storaro's virtuoso camera captures him from a vantage outside the airport terminal and follows in a perfectly designed tracking shot. It is more than a beautiful shot; it is an act of beautiful imagination. But *One from the Heart* makes it clear that it cannot escape beautiful imagination, that there can be no adequation of material reality to such imagination. This is why Frannie's job at the travel agency is to dress the windows as imagined destinations—in a central instance, a Bora Bora of the mind. "It's gonna be Bora Bora," she says when asked what her window diorama is going to be. "Bora Bora doesn't look like that," protests Ray (Raúl Juliá). "That's not the color of the sky." One standpoint from which to analyze the movie is its color design. In his role as consultant, Gene Kelly said that the plan was to use color the way it was in MGM's musicals. "We're going to *paint* the picture," he said.[238] The movie aspired to Technicolor, that is, which very much was a technology with its own content. Stanley Cavell has theorized that such color was used "to unify the projected world in another way than by direct reliance upon, or implication toward, the spatial-temporal consistency of the real world."[239] The content of Technicolor was the establishment of a "world of private fantasy," Cavell says, but this is complicated in *One from the Heart* because it is not 1950s Technicolor but the simulation of it. The ratio obtaining between private fantasy and public world in the 1950s, whether balanced or not, is not the same in this Zoetrope musical but is rather the object of nostalgic longing. Having failed to modernize corporate form, Coppola began to think of Zoetrope in a reimagined studio Hollywood. "There's no one like Zanuck around anymore, and there are no studios like there used to be," Coppola said. "I can envision Zoetrope being that way."[240]

It would be wrong, though, to call *One from the Heart* a nostalgia film, as Jameson treats the phenomenon. It may be an apt description of Coppola's subsequent movies, *Rumble Fish* and *Peggy Sue Got Married*. But *One from the Heart* functions more like a desublimation of the musical's critique, as D. A. Miller has understood it. Like the musical, *One from the Heart* defies "the concept of the so-called integrated show" and pursues instead "not the integration of drama and music found on the thematic surface, but a so much deeper formal discontinuity between the two that no makeshift for reconciling them could ever make the transition from one to the other less abrupt, or more plausible."[241] The discontinuity in Coppola's movie is that Hank cannot perform the fantasy he can project. Perhaps no one can. But denying us a performer of Gene Kelly's caliber at the center of this self-styled musical withholds from us even the transcendent moment of performance. "The true content of show-tune transcendence," Miller claims, "is simply the strength to endure a depressive status quo," which is why its rarefied performance comes off as an "otherworldy asylum" available to us only as "show business."[242] Hence Hank and Frannie are offered the false promise of entertainers, he the circus girl Leila (Nastassja Kinski), and she the piano player Ray, entertainers whose only virtue is that they evanesce so readily and never present the obstinacy of a "depressive status quo." Leila states this plainly enough. "If you want to get rid of a circus girl, all you gotta do is close your eyes," she says. "Then she disappears." Leila disappears shortly after, not with the aid of a cut, nothing like a Méliès vanishing, but through an act of framing: the camera first holds Leila in a long shot but then reframes to include Hank and tracks forward with him as he walks away, his figure eclipsing hers. And then she is gone. Evanescent, like a song.

One from the Heart is about imagination and its upshot. It is about the immiscibility of imagination and real life, of the image and its material infrastructure. In effect, it is about how much it takes to finance a fleeting image. Those sold on Coppola's vision of an electronic cinema would make bombastic claims that Hollywood should pay Coppola back for the so-called excesses of *One from the Heart* because, not excesses at all, they were rather a form of research and development that Hollywood lacked the foresight to make for itself. Coppola invited such rhetoric. "The motion picture technology used today is the first technology that we ever came up with," he said. "And the cameras that were made in 1920 and 1940, or ones just like them, are still turning in every studio today."[243]

In a recent study on digital cinema, Stephen Prince says that Coppola and Lucas were the two early figures of the digital revolution, but that Lucas's Industrial Light and Magic displayed more practical commitment in the development of its infrastructure. While Coppola cared to rattle Hollywood infrastructure, he seemed more concerned to imagine what superstructure might assemble itself on a new technological base. *One from the Heart* is an assessment of the habits of imagination in relation to the going resources of imagination. Outstripping Hollywood's old technology, Coppola said, meant that we'd no longer be doomed to think mechanically; we'd no longer be beholden, one infers, to Fordism. The creative process, Coppola argued, is rather "a series of thoughts and impressions that kind of come out all at once—not one, two, three, four, five, [but] almost the way a Polaroid picture develops before your eyes."[244] If "liberated from the mechanical tools," he believes the effect would be the revelation of imagination as "a kind of spatial process."[245]

Formally, this is what we find at work in *One from the Heart*. Consider, as one example, the early scene of Hank in the apartment of his friend, Moe (Harry Dean Stanton), with the two men sitting on the couch commiserating. Suddenly, through a scrim lighting effect, the tapestry behind them turns transparent and gives onto the scene of Frannie in the apartment of her friend, Maggie (Lainie Kazan). We

Rather than using a cut, *One from the Heart*
stages separate spaces on a single set.

watch the two women discuss Frannie's breakup, over the shoulders,
as it were, of Hank and Moe, in the shared space of a single set. As in
the previous example of Leila's disappearance, the change is achieved
without a cut. More like live theater than cinema, we traverse space
without regard for the temporality, governed by machines, that had
once given film narrative its structure. The shift from temporality to
spatiality is signaled in Tom Waits's soundtrack lyric: "Knowing that you
fall in love once upon a *town.*" This shift, as we'll see in Sofia Coppola's
cinema, has real consequences. No longer does narrative connection
hold sway—a fact disclosed here in Hank and Frannie's story being too
routine to need conclusion—and what fills its structuring function is a
new propulsion given by spectacle, assembled and reassembled right
before our eyes.

What we find in *One from the Heart,* in short, is Sofia Coppola's
cinema foretold. One can map various paths between Francis and Sofia
Coppola's cinema, and for that matter between theirs and Roman Coppola's cinema. They all share the sound designer, Richard Beggs, and

as my argument attests, sound design is a key feature in their cinema. Songs matter. One rather obscure connection is the Elvis Costello song. Mary Corleone had listened to Elvis Costello in her Sicilian villa, and in Sofia's *Lost in Translation* (2003), during a night of karaoke, Bill Murray sings Elvis Costello's "(What's So Funny 'bout) Peace, Love, and Understanding."

The connection is germane, I suggest, because the post-punk canon would become the soundtrack to Sofia's *Marie Antoinette,* perhaps her most important work to date. That movie begins with the most unlikely anachronism. Kirsten Dunst, onetime Virgin Suicide now dolled-up as Marie Anoinette, luxuriates in a room within the Palace of Versailles (the *real* Palace of Versailles, to which Sofia gained unprecedented access) to the score of Gang of Four's "Natural's Not in It." The anachronism works at different levels. The problem, at its most basic, is that the pop song is not a musical form for Marie Antoinette. The music she hears is parlor-room piano with the female voice for accompaniment, say, or the Paris Opera. Beyond this historical disagreement, though, there is anachronism of another kind, concerned with what has been called "structure of feeling." The Gang of Four lyrics ask, "The problem of leisure / What to do for pleasure?" The problem the song confronts is the problem of commodity structure, an organization of social relations that makes "ideal love, a new purchase." And the irony is that Gang of Four takes on this problem in the pop song, the ideal musical form of commodity culture. The commodity is the problem hanging over the age of the bourgeoisie, of course, and Marie Antoinette is still an aristocrat. The movie prefers her, nonetheless, as the archetype of pop-song sensibility.

What this sensibility entails had been the object of Sofia's first feature, *The Virgin Suicides.* And there the pop song had a built-in purpose, given it by Jeffrey Eugenides in his source novel: It was the line of communication between the shut-away Lisbon girls and the neighborhood boys, "diary entries the girls whispered" into their ears.[246] Sofia Coppola's cinema explicates pop-song sensibility, from *The Virgin Suicides* on. We might describe this sensibility, as opera might see it, as one wherein all pleasure is interiorized at the expense of society. No plausible relation can be thought to obtain, henceforth, between one's inner splendor and the outer dowdiness of the world.

This can be understood variously. One important takeaway, though, is that Sofia's cinema defeats narrative, insofar as it can be defined as the act of connecting oneself to society beyond. With *Marie Antoinette,* Sofia Coppola took the flatness of Mary Corleone's affect and reconfigured it into flattened plot trajectory. Marie Antoinette, as presented, sees no relationship between her desire, sealed off so thoroughly by royal protocol, and the social life of the masses outside the palace walls. The movie does not work, that is, as historical fiction. It depicts rather a total diremption of private and public itineraries, as experienced from Marie Antoinette's standpoint. The critic Nathan Lee argues that this, the real world's remove from Versailles, leads to the movie's "only serious mistake" in the form of "an extension of the narrative beyond [Marie Antoinette's] frame of reference." It doesn't make sense, in other words, to see "the storming of Versailles," not from her perspective at any rate, and here the movie becomes "nearly incoherent on a narrative level."[247] I agree with Lee's description, but not as an evaluation. This narrative incoherence is not a flaw but simply the effect of the pop-song's hermeticism in confrontation with the flow of history. We experience no final catharsis when she must flee Versailles, and that, I would venture, is because tragedy belongs to opera, not pop songs. Pop songs deal with euphoria and its absence. Much of Marie Antoinette's life, in Sofia Coppola's hands, plays like a music video, euphoric but self-contained and transient.

Nowhere is this better illustrated than in the scene of her feeling oppressed within Versailles, her husband Louis XVI complacent and happy to play cards with palace guests. "Don't you want to go to Paris, see the opera?" she asks him. "I'm more comfortable just to stay here," he responds. "We have everything we need." On the one hand, this speaks to the satiety of a king, on the other hand to the royal deprivation of society. Denied the opera, Marie gazes out the window and imagines her lover, Count Fersen, looking oddly Napoleonic on horseback. She excuses herself, caught up as she is in fantasy, and runs down palace halls, her footsteps coordinated with the staccato rhythms of the Strokes' "What Ever Happened?" The remainder of the song is scored to a jump-cut montage of Marie lying on her bed daydreaming, *pace* Louis XVI, about the things she needs but does not have. The interlude could be mistaken for a music video.

Marie Antoinette claps at the Paris Opera. |

In a visual rhyme, Marie Antoinette
confronts the masses. |

If Sofia Coppola's cinema might be characterized as music video in serial form, then we ought to consider how well this describes Francis Ford Coppola's *One from the Heart.* Sofia's movies tend to have scores from pop bands, such as Air's soundtrack for *The Virgin Suicides* and Phoenix's score for *Somewhere* (2010). This is the formula, too, for *One from the Heart,* and while it might resemble MGM's songbook musicals

(Gershwin songs, Freed and Brown songs), it bears closer likeness to what is called the jukebox musical (*Rock around the Clock* [1956] and *A Hard Day's Night* [1964]). This was a form ascendant in the 1960s, a famous example being *The Graduate* (1967), which plays to the songs of Simon and Garfunkel. Coppola had himself worked in this form in his first feature, *You're a Big Boy Now*, which used the songs of the Lovin' Spoonful for its soundtrack. One sees how this would have benefited entertainment conglomerates, who could sell the same audience both the movie and its soundtrack. There is in this, though, a principle of formal breakdown, with the songs pulling against the larger unity of the movie. This, I have argued, was the disunity threatening the corporate conglomerate, too, and the value in considering Coppola's career in historical perspective is that we see his corporation, American Zoetrope, offered up as a business idea that might counteract the tendencies built in to the corporation otherwise. The opera, I have argued too, was an aesthetic rendering of corporate form construed in unitary terms. Opera cedes to pop song in the Coppola family cinema, and this tradeoff gives what we might call American Zoetrope 2.0 its new aesthetic. In 2007 Francis Ford Coppola gave full ownership of American Zoetrope to his children, Roman and Sofia, only officializing a transition begun with *One from the Heart*. Their generation of directors, nearly to the person, cut their teeth directing music videos. Roman did. Sofia did. Sofia's first husband, Spike Jonze, did. This, for better or worse, is the outcome of New Hollywood.

Notes

1. Peter Cowie, *Coppola* (New York: Da Capo Press, 1994), 6; and Bruce Handy, "The Liberation of Francis Ford Coppola," *Vanity Fair*, December 2007, accessed April 9, 2014, http://www.vanityfair.com/culture/features/2007/12/coppola200712.

2. Dwight Macdonald, "A Theory of Mass Culture," in *Mass Culture*, ed. Bernard Rosenberg and David Manning White (New York: The Free Press, 1957), 65.

3. See Janet Wasko, *Movies and Money* (Norwood, N.J.: Ablex Publishing, 1982), in particular chapter 1 on D. W. Griffith's career in relation to banks and chapter 2 on the increased financial control of the film industry in the period 1927–39.

4. For one account, see Thomas Schatz, *The Genius of the System* (Minneapolis: University of Minnesota Press, 2010), 29–35.

5. Macdonald, "Theory of Mass Culture," 65.

6. See Thomas Frank, *The Conquest of Cool* (Chicago: University of Chicago Press, 1997); Rosabeth Moss Kanter, *The Change Masters* (New York: Simon and Schuster, 1983); and Art Kleiner, *The Age of Heretics* (New York: Doubleday, 1996).

7. Fred Turner, *From Counterculture to Cyberculture* (Chicago: University of Chicago Press, 2006). Turner presses against a standard argument that "the authentically revolutionary ideals of the generation of 1968 were somehow co-opted by the forces they opposed" to argue instead that "the same military-industrial research world that brought forth nuclear weapons—and computers—also gave rise to a free-wheeling, interdisciplinary, and highly entrepreneurial style of work" (4). Stewart Brand, Turner shows, has long proselytized the latter values in the name of the counterculture.

8. Chris Nashawaty, *Crab Monsters, Teenage Cavemen, and Candy Stripe Nurses* (New York: Harry N. Abrams, 2013), 59 (the director Jack Hill makes the remark).

9. See *A Legacy of Filmmakers: The Early Years of American Zoetrope*, a documentary included on the *THX-1138* DVD (Warner Home Video, 2004).

10. Ibid.

11. Michael Ondaatje, *The Conversations* (New York: Alfred A. Knopf, 2011), 15.

12. Turner, *From Counterculture to Cyberculture*, 4.

13. Manuel Castells and Alejandro Portes, "World Underneath: The Origins, Dynamics, and Effects of the Informal Economy," in *The Informal Economy*, ed. Alejandro Portes, Manuel Castells, and Lauren A. Benton (Baltimore: Johns Hopkins University Press, 1989), 25.

14. Michael Sragow, "Godfatherhood," in *Francis Ford Coppola Interviews*, ed. Gene D. Phillips and Rodney Hill (Jackson: University Press of Mississippi, 2004), 167.

15. Andrew Sarris, *The American Cinema: Directors and Directions, 1929–1968* (New York: E. P. Dutton and Co., 1968), 31, 37.

16. Coppola says this on the audio commentary for the *The Godfather* DVD (Paramount, 2001).

17. Eleanor Coppola, *Notes on a Life* (New York: Doubleday, 2008), 19.

18. Douglas McGregor, "The Human Side of Enterprise," *Management Review* 46.1 (1957): 22.

19. Pauline Kael, *Raising Kane* (London: Methuen, 2002), 131–32.

20. Dan Simons, "Francis Ford Coppola and American Zoetrope," *Entertainment World*, March 27, 1970, 17.

21. Michael Pye and Lynda Myles, *The Movie Brats: How the Film Generation Took over Hollywood* (New York: Holt, Rinehart, and Winston, 1979), 81.

22. William Murray, "*Playboy* Interview: Francis Ford Coppola," in *Francis Ford Coppola Interviews*, ed. Gene D. Phillips and Rodney Hill (Jackson: University Press of Mississippi, 2004), 39.

23. See Murray Smith, "Theses on the Philosophy of Hollywood History," in *Contemporary Hollywood Cinema*, ed. Steve Neale and Murray Smith (London: Routledge, 1998), 3–20. Smith objects to Michael Storper's descriptions of Hollywood's transition from Fordism into post-Fordism, in particular the equivocation that "because films are not absolutely identical—two formulaic genre films still have many more significant differences than do two cars of the same model, produced on an assembly line—the 'Fordist' nature of the mode of production in the studio era was always somewhat compromised" (7–8).

24. I refer here to Janet Staiger's sections "The Hollywood Mode of Production to 1930" (85–154) and "The Hollywood Mode of Production, 1930–1960" (309–38) from the well-known larger study authored jointly by David Bordwell, Janet Staiger, and Kristin Thompson, *The Classical Hollywood Cinema* (New York: Columbia University Press, 1985).

25. Bordwell, Staiger, and Thompson, *Classical Hollywood Cinema*, 109, 90.

26. Ibid., 121.

27. Ibid., 135, 119.

28. Ibid., 135.

29. John Ford qtd. in Bill Grantham, "Embracing Jurisdiction: John Ford's *The Man Who Shot Liberty Valance*," in *Jurisprudence of Jurisdiction*, ed. Shaun McVeigh (New York: Routledge-Cavendish, 2007), 225.

30. Shyon Baumann, *Hollywood Highbrow* (Princeton, N.J.: Princeton University Press, 2007), 60. Ford liked to call it a "job of work," Baumann argues, in an effort not to intellectualize it.

31. Michael Schumacher, *Francis Ford Coppola* (New York: Crown Publishers, 1999), 3.

32. Cowie, *Coppola*, 11.

33. See David Harvey, *The Condition of Postmodernity* (Oxford: Wiley-Blackwell, 1991), 121–97. Harvey defines this term of analysis derived from "regulation school" economics. I owe the phrase "unleashing capitalism" to Andrew Glyn, namely his study, *Capitalism Unleashed* (Oxford: Oxford University Press, 2006), which continues to strike me as one of the more lucid accounts of the economic transition under discussion here.

34. Harriet Rubin, "Art of Darkness," *Fast Company* 18 (October 1998): 136.

35. Peter F. Drucker, "Henry Ford: Success and Failure," *Harper's Magazine* 195.116 (July 1947): 4.

36. Ibid.

37. Ibid., 5.

38. Ibid., 7.

39. Ibid., 1.

40. Rubin, "Art of Darkness."

41. Ibid.

42. Simons, "Francis Ford Coppola," 17.

43. Cowie, *Coppola*, 57.

44. Rubin, "Art of Darkness," 136.

45. Peter Drucker, *The Practice of Management* (New York: Harper and Row, 1954), 36.

46. Ibid., 37.

47. Murray, "*Playboy* Interview," 39.

48. Cowie, *Coppola*, 216.

49. Gerald Nachman, "Coppola of Zoetrope—Older, Wiser and Poorer," *Los Angeles Times*, November 7, 1971, 57.

50. Handy, "Liberation of Francis Ford Coppola."

51. This description of New York City's turn to finance capital is offered by Fredric Jameson, "The Brick and the Balloon," in *The Cultural Turn: Selected Writings on the Postmodern, 1983–1998* (London: Verso, 1998), 167.

52. John Cutts, "The Dangerous Age," *Films and Filming* (May 1969): 10 (Pacific Film Archive, Berkeley, Calif.).

53. Tom Hayden, *The Port Huron Statement: The Visionary Call of the 1960s Revolution* (New York: Thunder's Mouth Press, 2005), 83.

54. See Claus Offe, *Disorganized Capitalism* (Cambridge: Massachusetts Institute of Techonology Press, 1985); and Scott Lash and John Urry, *The End of Organized Capitalism* (Madison: University of Wisconsin Press, 1987).

55. Francis Ford Coppola, "America's Talent Can Still Soar," Coppola files, Pacific Film Archive, Berkeley, Calif.

56. See Toby Miller, Nitin Govil, John McMurria, Ting Wang, and Richard Maxwell, *Global Hollywood 2* (London: British Film Institute Publishing, 2005).

57. Giovanni Arrighi, *The Long Twentieth Century* (London: Verso, 1994), 7.

58. See *Legacy of Filmmakers*.

59. See Eleanor Coppola, *Notes* (New York: Limelight Editions, 2001), 27.

60. See "*THX 1138*—Made in San Francisco," in *George Lucas Interviews*, ed. Sally Kline (Jackson: University Press of Mississippi, 1999), 8–13. There Lucas explains his aesthetic motivation: "My primary purpose in approaching the production of *THX-1138* was to make a kind of *cinema verité* of the future. However, I wanted it to look like a very slick, studied documentary in terms of technique. I come from a background of graphics, photography, art and painting—and I'm very graphics-conscious" (10).

61. Ibid.

62. For the story of Coppola bringing a generator into the village of Baler, see Coppola, *Notes*, 62. For Miriam Hansen's political take on *Apocalypse Now*, see "Traces of Transgression in *Apocalypse Now*," *Social Text* 3 (Autumn 1980): 127.

63. David A. Cook, *Lost Illusions: American Cinema in the Shadow of Watergate and Vietnam, 1970–1979*, vol. 9 of *History of the American Cinema* (New York: Charles Scribner's Sons, 2000), 303.

64. Cowie, *Coppola*, 24–25.

65. Ibid., 25.

66. Ibid., 24.

67. Joseph Gelmis, "Francis Ford Coppola: Free Agent within the System," in *Francis Ford Coppola Interviews*, ed. Gene D. Phillips and Rodney Hill (Jackson: University Press of Mississippi, 2004), 12.

68. Hayden, *Port Huron Statement*, 84.

69. Ibid., 72, 46.

70. See *Legacy of Filmmakers*.

71. Francis Ford Coppola, audio commentary on *Finian's Rainbow* DVD (Warner Home Video, 2005).

72. Stephen Farber, "George Lucas: The Stinky Kid Hits the Big Time," in *George Lucas Interviews*, ed. Sally Kline (Jackson: University Press of Mississippi, 1999), 36.

73. Murray, "*Playboy* Interview," 37.

74. Ibid., 38.

75. Gene D. Phillips, *Godfather* (Lexington: University Press of Kentucky, 2004), 54.

76. Cowie, *Coppola*, 48.

77. Betty Friedan, *The Feminine Mystique* (New York: W. W. Norton and Co., 1997).

78. Ibid., 21.

79. Ibid., 50.

80. Ibid., 30.

81. Daniel Horowitz, *Betty Friedan and the Making of* The Feminine Mystique*: The American Left, the Cold War, and Modern Feminism* (Amherst: University of Massachusetts Press, 1998), 3.

82. Phillips, *Godfather*, 56.

83. Dan Simons, "'Rain People' by Rule Breaker," *Los Angeles Times*, September 9, 1969 (Pacific Film Archive, Berkeley, Calif.).

84. Cowie, *Coppola*, 53.

85. See George Lucas's *Filmmaker*, a documentary of the making of *The Rain People*.

86. Bob Motley, "Two 'Godfathers' Are Better than One," *New Times*, May 3, 1974 (Pacific Film Archive, Berkeley, Calif.).

87. Phillips, *Godfather*, 58.

88. Louise Sweeney, "The Movie Business Is Alive and Well and Living in San Francisco," *Show* 1 (April 1970): 35.

89. Dennis Schaefer and Larry Salvato, *Masters of Light* (Berkeley: University of California Press, 1985), 90.

90. John Cutts, "The Dangerous Age," *Films and Filming* (May 1969): 8.

91. Cowie, *Coppola*, 46.

92. Ibid., 47.

93. Mathias Nilges, "The Anti-Anti-Oedipus: Representing Post-Fordist Subjectivity," *Mediations* 23.2 (Spring 2008): 32, 31.

94. Phillips, *Godfather,* 59.

95. Ibid., 55.

96. Ibid, 53.

97. Ibid., 52.

98. Gilles Deleuze, *Cinema 1: The Movement-Image,* trans. Hugh Tomlinson and Barbara Habberjam (Minneapolis: University of Minnesota Press, 1986), 71–80.

99. Ibid., 58, 59, 61.

100. Ibid., 61.

101. Ibid., 62.

102. Ibid., 77.

103. Ibid., 78.

104. Ibid., 77.

105. Ibid., 78.

106. Ibid., 81.

107. Ibid., 58.

108. We find something of the same thing in Jean-François Lyotard's *The Postmodern Condition,* trans. Geoff Bennington and Brian Massumi (Minneapolis: University of Minnesota Press, 1993), although when Lyotard uses the comparable term "open system," he more forthrightly does the work of applying it not only to science, which is his model of knowledge, but to the operations of political economy (64).

109. Deleuze, *Cinema 1,* 17.

110. Simons, "'Rain People' by Rule Breaker."

111. "S.F. Film Craft Union Gives Coppola Full Control in Return for 55-Hr. Week," *Variety,* September 24, 1969 (Pacific Film Archive, Berkeley, Calif.).

112. Ibid.

113. Sweeney, "Movie Business Is Alive and Well," 36.

114. Simons, "'Rain People' by Rule Breaker."

115. Cutts, "Dangerous Age," 6.

116. Simons, "Francis Ford Coppola," 15.

117. Ibid., 17.

118. Ibid.

119. Ibid.

120. Cutts, "Dangerous Age," 5.

121. Ondaatje, *Conversations,* 15.

122. Simons, "Francis Ford Coppola," 17.

123. Nachman, "Coppola of Zoetrope," 57.

124. Coppola, *Notes on a Life,* 257.

125. Murray, "*Playboy* Interview," 19.

126. Ibid., 27.

127. Schumacher, *Francis Ford Coppola,* 85.

128. John Micklethwait and Adrian Wooldridge, *The Company* (New York: Random House, 2003), 120.

129. Ibid., 96.

130. See *Berkeley in the Sixties,* dir. Mark Kitchell, DVD (First Run Features, 2002).

131. Jon Lewis, *The Godfather* (London: Palgrave Macmillan, 2010), 25.

132. David Thompson, "Michael Corleone, Role Model: Celebrating a Quarter Century of Killer Executive Style," *Esquire* 127.3 (March 1997): 60–62.

133. See Paul Potter, "We Must Name the System," Speech delivered at March on Washington in April 1965, in *The Sixties Papers: Documents of a Rebellious Decade,* ed. Judith Clavier Albert and Stewart Edward Albert (New York: Praeger, 1984), 219–25. Paul Potter was then president of SDS.

134. See Carl Oglesby, *The Yankee and Cowboy War* (New York: Berkley Publishing Group, 1977); and Richard Kaufman, "As Eisenhower Was Saying . . . 'We Must Guard against Unwarranted Influence by the Military-Industrial Complex,'" in *The Corporation in the American Economy,* ed. Harry M. Trebing (Chicago: Quadrangle Books, 1970), 43–59.

135. This story gets repeated in many places. Paramount executives were resolutely against casting Brando as Vito, largely because Brando had a reputation for being undependable. One of the conditions they set on his casting, therefore, was that he consent to a screen test, which they were sure would be a great enough indignity for an actor of his stature as to bar his accepting the role. Coppola, the story goes, got around this by doing an unconventional screen test, one that did not feel at all like auditioning, and during this screen test Brando was said to have physically transformed himself so impressively—by painting his hair with shoe polish and filling his cheeks with wads of Kleenex—that Paramount executives were able to see him as right for the Don. For one version of this, see Murray, "*Playboy* Interview," 22.

136. Ronald Coase, "The Nature of the Firm," in *The Nature of the Firm,* ed. Oliver E. Williamson and Sidney G. Winter (New York: Oxford University Press, 1991), 19, 20.

137. Ibid., 19.

138. Fredric Jameson, "Reification and Utopia in Mass Culture," in *Signatures of the Visible* (New York: Routledge, 1992), 32.

139. Ibid.

140. Ibid., 33.

141. G. W. F. Hegel, *Philosophy of Right,* trans. T. M. Knox (London: Oxford University Press, 1967), 110.

142. Alfred D. Chandler Jr., *Scale and Scope: The Dynamics of Industrial Capitalism* (Cambridge, Mass.: Harvard University Press, 1990), part 3, "Personal Capitalism," 235–392.

143. Ibid., 240.

144. Ibid., 243.

145. Charles Dellheim, "The Creation of a Company Culture: Cadburys," *American Historical Review* 92.1 (February 1987): 14. See also Christopher Smith, John Child, and Michael Rowlinson, *Reshaping Work: The Cadbury Experience* (Cambridge: Cambridge University Press, 1990), 50–57.

146. Hegel, *Philosophy of Right,* 115.

147. Ibid., 114.

148. Robert Scheer and Susan Lyne, "An Interview with Francis Ford Coppola," *City of San Francisco,* December 2, 1975, 21 (emphasis added).

149. Peter Bart, "Three's Company," *Variety,* December 6, 2004 (Coppola files, Pacific Film Archive, Berkeley, Calif.).

150. See Jon Lewis, *Whom God Wishes to Destroy* (Durham, N.C.: Duke University Press, 1996), 15–17, and Schumacher, *Francis Ford Coppola,* 180–82.

151. Bart, "Three's Company."

152. Ibid.

153. Handy, "Liberation of Francis Ford Coppola."

154. Schumacher, *Francis Ford Coppola,* 182.

155. Claire Clouzot, "The Morning of the Magician: George Lucas and *Star Wars,*" in *George Lucas Interviews,* ed. Sally Kline (Jackson: University Press of Mississippi, 1999), 62.

156. Jean Valley, "*The Empire Strikes Back* and So Does Filmmaker George Lucas with His Sequel to *Star Wars,*" in *George Lucas Interviews,* ed. Sally Kline (Jackson: University Press of Mississippi, 1999), 96.

157. Clouzot, "Morning of the Magician," 63.

158. Valley, "*Empire Strikes Back,*" 96.

159. Schumacher, *Francis Ford Coppola,* 375.

160. Valley, "*Empire Strikes Back,*" 97.

161. Robert Lindsey, "Francis Ford Coppola: Promises to Keep," *New York Times Magazine,* July 24, 1988, 27.

162. See Lewis, *Whom God Wishes to Destroy,* 153. It should be noted that in referring to Capra's "peculiar populism," Lewis means to vouch for Lucas's hunch that such populism "would play well in conservative 1980s America" (153). Lewis thinks rather that Coppola's aesthetic uptake of the Capra themes compromised Lucas's plan, and in what follows I will agree with Lewis's assessment.

163. Ibid., 152.

164. See Jon Lewis, "The Perfect Money Machine(s): George Lucas, Steven Spielberg, and Auteurism in the New Hollywood," in *Looking Past the Screen,* ed. Jon Lewis and Eric Smoodin (Durham, N.C.: Duke University Press, 2007), 68.

165. Rex Weiner, "Lucas the Loner Returns to *Wars,*" in *George Lucas Interviews,* ed. Sally Kline (Jackson: University Press of Mississippi, 1999), 187.

166. Lewis, *Whom God Wishes to Destroy,* 153.

167. Lindsey, "Francis Ford Coppola," 23.

168. Ibid., 27.

169. Stuart Klawans, "Tucker: The Man and His Dream," *The Nation* 247.7 (September 26, 1988): 250.

170. Ibid.

171. See J. D. Connor, *The Studios after the Studios: Neoclassical Hollywood, 1970–2010* (Stanford, Calif.: Stanford University Press, forthcoming), chap. 1.

172. Terrence Rafferty, "Tucker: The Man and His Dream," *New Yorker* 64.27 (August 22, 1998): 62.

173. See the director's commentary track, *Tucker: A Man and His Dreams*, DVD (Paramount, 2000).

174. See Jay David Bolter and Richard Grusin, *Remediation* (Cambridge: Massachusetts Institute of Technology Press, 1999).

175. Lewis, "Perfect Money Machine(s)," 68.

176. Rafferty, "Tucker," 63.

177. Hansen, "Traces of Transgression," 127.

178. Ibid., 128.

179. *Hearts of Darkness* DVD (Lionsgate, 2010).

180. Cowie, *Coppola*, 8, 20.

181. Karen Monson, "Coppola Directs American Premier of 'The Visit,'" *Los Angeles Herald-Examiner*, October 31, 1972, C-4.

182. See Coppola, *Notes*, 68–69.

183. Ivan Nagel, *Autonomy and Mercy* (Cambridge, Mass.: Harvard University Press, 1991).

184. Ibid., 6, 4.

185. Ibid., 6.

186. Joseph Kerman, *Opera as Drama* (Berkeley: University of California Press, 1988), 19.

187. Nagel, *Autonomy and Mercy*, 26. This magic is invoked to heal "the ruptures of the new era and the disruption of the old," Nagel says, "the rift in time" between the absolutist state and republican governance, which is rendered by *Die Zauberflöte* as the "split world of good and evil" and then overcome by magic (17–22). The opera was an "unprecedented success." In 1794 the *Journal des Luxus und der Moden* wrote, "Something that can have this effect on an entire nation must certainly be one of the most potent fermentation," and Nagel explains its effect precisely in terms of its "propaganda potential" (22).

188. Ibid., 157.

189. Ibid., 158.

190. Ibid., 177.

191. Ibid., 157.

192. Juliet Koss, *Modernism after Wagner* (Minneapolis: University of Minnesota Press, 2010), xiii.

193. Friedrich Nietzsche, *The Birth of Tragedy and the Case of Wagner*, trans. Walter Kaufmann (New York: Vintage, 1967), 167.

194. Jean-Paul Sartre, "Why Write?" in *What Is Literature?*, trans. Bernard Frechtman (London: Routledge, 2001), 43.

195. See Arthur Machen, "Corporate Personality," *Harvard Law Review* 24.4 (1911): 253–67. This article is famously the first effort to asses German jurisprudence on corporate personality from the perspective of common law. It surveys a range of German jurists including Friedrich Karl von Savigny, Alois von Brinz, Otto von Gierke, and Ernst Zitelman.

196. Ibid., x.

197. Nietzsche, *Birth of Tragedy and the Case of Wagner*, 103.

198. Hansen, "Traces of Transgression," 125.

199. Greil Marcus, "Journey Up the River: An Interview with Francis Ford Coppola," *Rolling Stone*, November 1, 1979, 55.

200. Hansen, "Traces of Transgression," 131.

201. Coppola, *Notes*, 52.

202. Ivan Kreilkamp, "A Voice without a Body: The Phonographic Logic of *Heart of Darkness*," *Victorian Studies* 40.2 (Winter 1997): 213.

203. Cowie, *Coppola*, 8.

204. Francis Ford Coppola, "A Memo from Francis Ford Coppola," *Esquire* 88.5 (November 1977): 190.

205. Ibid., 195.

206. Ibid., 190.

207. Ibid., 194.

208. Ibid., 194.

209. Ibid., 194–195, 196.

210. Ibid., 194.

211. Michal Grover-Friedlander, *Vocal Apparitions: The Attraction of Cinema to Opera* (Princeton, N.J.: Princeton University Press, 2005), 133. For Adorno's discussion of Wagner's repudiation of Orpheus, see *In Search of Wagner* (London: Verso, 2009), 113.

212. Ibid.

213. Slavoj Žižek, *Tarrying with the Negative* (Durham, N.C.: Duke University Press, 1993), 166.

214. Sragow, "Godfatherhood," 169.

215. Schumacher, *Francis Ford Coppola*, 415.

216. Ibid., 414.

217. My study-in-progress, *Art's Economy: Post-Fordist Cinema and Hollywood Counterculture, 1962–1975*, attempts something along just these lines. In it, I narrate a cultural history of such new corporations as Kirk Douglas's Bryna Productions, Robert Altman's Lion's Gate, the Zanuck/Brown Company, and BBS Productions, with reference as well to the first iteration of American Zoetrope and the outlier enterprises of John Cassavetes.

218. In one interview, Coppola claims, "I'm no longer dependent on the movie business to make a living. So if I want to make movies as other old guys would play golf, I can." See Handy, "Liberation of Francis Ford Coppola," 252.

219. Sragow, "Godfatherhood," 169.

220. Handy, "Liberation of Francis Ford Coppola," 252.

221. Rubin, "Art of Darkness," 134.

222. Benedict Carver, "New Dreams for Zoetrope," *Variety*, July 20, 1998, 7.

223. Larry Rohter, "Family Dynamics, without the Bullets," *New York Times*, June 3, 2009, 18.

224. Richard Corliss, "Coppola's *Tetro*: An Offer You Can Refuse," *Time*, June 11, 2009, accessed February 20, 2014, http://content.time.com/time/arts/article/0,8599,1904079,00.html.

225. Lewis, *Whom God Wishes to Destroy*, 147.

226. Ondaatje, *Conversations*, 156.

227. Lewis, *Whom God Wishes to Destroy*, 147.

228. Corliss, "Coppola's *Tetro*."

229. Cowie, *Coppola*, 39.

230. Simons, "Francis Ford Coppola," 17. Early on, this was Coppola's claim—that he "knew the guys"—over against the establishment. In George Lucas's *Filmmaker*, in the middle of a testy phone call, Coppola says, "I don't need the unions, because I know the guys who can make the picture just as well, and in some instances better, than the craftsmen who are unionized."

231. Michael Ventura, "Coppola Woes and the Zoetrope Revolution," *L.A. Weekly*, February 13, 1981, 8.

232. David Denby's criticism that the "day Francis Coppola abandoned realism for artifice has to rank among the saddest in film history" is quoted by Lewis, *Whom God Wishes to Destroy*, 144. Peter Cowie, too, notes this bifurcation in Coppola's career, though not in terms of realism and artifice. He claims that Coppola's Academy Award presentation in April 1979, when he speechified on the digital revolution, was his peak moment, after which "critics and audiences have confessed to a feeling if not of betrayal then of frustrated expectation where Coppola is concerned" (Cowie, *Coppola* 145).

233. Lillian Ross, "Some Figures on a Fantasy: Francis Coppola," in *Francis Ford Coppola Interviews*, ed. Gene D. Phillips and Rodney Hill (Jackson: University Press of Mississippi, 2004), 64.

234. Ibid., 65.

235. This quotes Francis Ford Coppola in the liner notes of a CD soundtrack of *One from the Heart* restored and remastered in 2004.

236. Scott Haller, "Francis Ford Coppola's Biggest Gamble: *One from the Heart*," in *Francis Ford Coppola Interviews*, ed. Gene D. Phillips and Rodney Hill (Jackson: University Press of Mississippi, 2004), 60.

237. Ross, "Some Figures on a Fantasy," 67.

238. Ibid., 75.

239. Stanley Cavell, *The World Viewed* (Cambridge, Mass.: Harvard University Press, 1979), 81.

240. Haller, "Francis Ford Coppola's Biggest Gamble," 54.

241. D. A. Miller, *Place for Us: Essay on the Broadway Musical* (Cambridge, Mass.: Harvard University Press, 1998), 3.

242. Ibid., 7–8.

243. Ventura, "Coppola Woes and the Zoetrope Revolution," 7.

244. Paula Parisi, "A Conversation with Francis Ford Coppola," *American Cinematographer* 72.8 (August 1991): 71.

245. Ibid.

246. Jeffrey Eugenides, *The Virgin Suicides* (New York: Picador, 1993), 190.

247. Nathan Lee, "Pretty Vacant," *Film Comment* 42.5 (September 1, 2006): 25.

Interview with Francis Ford Coppola |

This interview was conducted by e-mail in December 2013.

JEFF MENNE: The party line on you has been that you were too much an artist to be a good businessperson. But it seems history will tell a different story—that is, that you have been responsible for creating different business models perhaps more than any other filmmaker in your generation. Do you think your artistic sense has opposed your business sense, or has it complemented it?

FRANCIS FORD COPPOLA: I always had good entrepreneurial instincts, even while a student in college; setting up and running the student drama organization and sparring with faculty was the basis of American Zoetrope. Later, my adventure buying the Hollywood General Studios and trying to set up a hybrid of the old-fashioned studio system fused with new technologies (Zoetrope Studios) was both a trauma and great learning experience. After barely surviving that adventure, and then having the opportunity to sit on the MGM-UA board for several years, it added up to a sort of business-school education. I reorganized my business interests (AZ, the wine business, publishing) and applied what I had learned—mainly insisting on one accounting system throughout. This gave me a way to move forward more sensibly and with a healthy fear of debt and banks. Nearly getting wiped out after *One from the Heart* was a shock, and so I proceeded in the later part of my life more carefully, keeping a constant eye on debt as well as recruiting a solid CEO to run business affairs. But to this day, the company is owned and run by an artist rather than a businessperson, which is unusual for this country.

JM: You made a point of starting American Zoetrope as not just a place where you could do your work, but where others could do their work. What kind of environment and what kind of ethos did you hope to create at American Zoetrope?

FFC: My experience at Hofstra College was formative. It was the first time I stayed in one school for more than eight months, and I was given wonderful opportunities as a theater major. I loved working shoulder to shoulder with the other students, mounting ambitious productions, building scenery, doing the lighting, and all the fraternization that comes with it. Graduate film school was very different—the different colleagues locked up alone in their editing rooms, monopolizing equipment, without the family-style experience that's part of theater. So American Zoetrope was a way to combine what I had learned from the theater with a film company—working with colleagues to make the films of our dreams.

JM: American Zoetrope might seem a failed venture, simply because Warner Bros. pulled their funding, but its legacy has been great, and as a business idea it has seemed to guide your career. And now you have left it for your children's careers. How do you now assess American Zoetrope?

FFC: Well, if one looks at a list of all the productions American Zoetrope made, those I directed and the many others that I did not, I think it shows a level of excellence, variety, and innovation that is a worthy legacy. We sponsored new filmmakers, reintroduced Jerry Lewis's concept of video assist, pioneered electronic editing, "previsualization," introduced the concept of "sound designer," brought back the performance of a live symphony orchestra with silent cinema, hired the first woman head of production (Lucy Fischer), aside from a filmography which includes a number of classics. And yes, now it is owned by my children (and grandchildren) who are all viable filmmakers in their own right.

JM: Looking back on the break with Warner Bros., how do you understand it? Was it just that *THX-1138* was too experimental? Was it a philosophical difference? It seems odd that John Calley was willing to stand by Stanley Kubrick, say, when he was taking risks and experimenting, but was so put off by *THX*.

FFC: We were located somewhere other than Los Angeles, and were not stylish or in vogue or certainly as established as Stanley Kubrick. John Calley was always a Hollywood phenomenon, despite his beard and U.K. sensibility, really no more intellectual than the other film executives. He wanted to be associated with the trendy and with winners, and we were only winners when viewed from later on.

JM: Since the 1960s, San Francisco has been the home of another pioneering industry—electronics—and of course the spirit of American Zoetrope was very open to technology. Were you affected by the parallel developments in that field, and the kinds of personalities attracted to that field?

FFC: I was always a kind of boy scientist, in love with science and technology, the only subject I was any good at. I began in theater with lighting, working for George Izenour, inventor of the electronic lighting board. So yes, being in San Francisco, George and I were very interested in visiting Xerox PARC (Palo Alto Research Center) to learn about their innovations to computing and where many of the things related to the internet and modern technology came from. Also American Zoetrope wanted to own and control its own filmmaking equipment; for example, American Zoetrope would sponsor a weekend each year in which we invited many of the companies to talk about what they were doing, then have all the sessions typed up and distributed to all, so we became a host and facilitator to new ideas.

JM: Your father was obviously a great musical influence on you, and your brother a great literary influence on you. Your work, hence, was from the outset coming from a tradition of the arts rather than solely from a Hollywood tradition. How has that shaped your personal theory on the relation of cinema and the other arts?

FFC: My father and brother were powerful influences in my artistic life. Our family was a hothouse experience in which you felt if you didn't have talent, you were dead. All the aspects of music theory, harmony, opera history and production, and its offspring the musical; literature, philosophy, semiology, aesthetics: I was always over my head, yet struggled to be in that universe.

JM: Opera, in particular, has seemed a strong influence on you all along. How has it shaped your aesthetic sensibility?

FFC: Well, I knew the stories of the operas, and I loved the workings of the stage, with its trapdoors, wind machines, and fly galleries; the mechanics and magic of the stories, the music, the dancing—all culminating in a thrilling experience. I think the era of the great virtuoso opera conductors (Wagner, von Bülow, Strauss, Mahler, etc.) were the forerunners of the filmmakers in that they were working in an enormously popular field, had their own artistic companies, and the final say over every aspect of the productions.

JM: With *One from the Heart,* some critics felt you had become "too formal," that the form had become more important than the content. People say this less often about literature, it seems—rarely are there complaints about sonnets and sestinas being too formal. What is your outlook on the form-content ratio, and what do you think of the critical appraisal that the ratio has shifted in your films in favor of form?

FFC: As I think back, I realize I had made *The Godfather, The Conversation, Godfather Part II,* and *Apocalypse Now* in short order, one after the other. I wanted to do something totally different in style and form, something with songs, like theater. Also, in my so-called mind, with my marriage failing, I imagined it would be part of a great four-part project based on Goethe's *Elective Affinities,* with its story related to the Man, the Woman, the Other Man, the Other Woman. To this day I am fascinated with form. I know I am filled with emotion; I just need the right envelope to put it in.

JM: In part I ask the last question because *One from the Heart* is a favorite of mine that seems to deserve a place with your other great works. Does it matter to you how your films have been rated?

FFC: Oh, I sort of failed my way up to success. I'm used to my films first being greeted with boos and am intrigued that they have been viewed so much more favorably later on. When I make a film now, I figure the real reaction will come in ten or twenty years. But of course it matters; when they don't like your film, it hurts your feelings. It's as though you worked on cooking a meal and everyone sat there at the table and hated it.

JM: With *Tetro* and *Twixt*, it's clear that personal content will always find a place in your films, though often it will show up in allegorical or other indirect ways. Why the indirection? Is there something in straight autobiographical content that doesn't compel you?

FFC: Although I feel that all one's work has to be somewhat about yourself, your life, and your understanding of contemporary life, it embarrasses me to be singled out as the focus. Throughout my life, the thing I am most frightened of is to be embarrassed in public. Maybe it comes from so often being the new kid in school, when all the eyes of the other students (the girls) were on you and to be ridiculed in front of them.

Dementia 13 (1963)
USA
Production: Roger Corman Productions
Producer: Francis Ford Coppola
Director: Francis Ford Coppola
Screenplay: Francis Ford Coppola
Photography: Charles Hannawalt
Art Director: Albert Locatelli
Editors: Mort Tubor and Stuart O'Brien
Music: Ronald Stein
Cast: William Campbell (Richard Haloran), Luana Anders (Louise Haloran),
    Bart Patton (Billy Haloran), Patrick Magee (Justin Caleb), Mary Mitchel
    (Kane), Ethne Dunn (Lady Haloran), Peter Reed (John Haloran), Barbara
    Dowling (Kathleen)
35 mm, black and white
75 min.

You're a Big Boy Now (1966)
USA
Production: Seven Arts
Producer: Phil Feldman
Director: Francis Ford Coppola
Screenplay: Francis Ford Coppola, based on the novel by David Benedictus
Photography: Andy Laszlo
Art Director: Vassele Fotopoulos
Costumes: Theoni V. Aldredge
Choreographer: Robert Tucker
Editor: Aram Avakian
Music: Bob Prince; Songs by John Sebastian; Performed by Lovin' Spoonful
Cast: Peter Kastner (Bernard Chanticleer), Elizabeth Hartman (Barbara Dar-
    ling), Geraldine Page (Margery Chanticleer), Julie Harris (Miss Thing), Rip
    Torn (I. H. Chanticleer), Tony Bill (Raef), Karen Black (Amy)

35 mm, color
96 min.

Finian's Rainbow (1968)
USA
Production: Warner Bros.–Seven Arts
Producer: Joseph Landon
Director: Francis Ford Coppola
Photography: Philip Lathrop
Production Designer: Hilyard M. Brown
Costumes: Dorothy Jenkins
Choreographer: Hermes Pan
Editor: Melvin Shapiro
Music Director: Ray Heindorf
Sound: M. A. Merrick and Dan Wallin
Cast: Fred Astaire (Finian McLonergan), Petula Clark (Sharon McLonergan),
    Tommy Steele (Og), Don Francks (Woody Mahoney), Barbara Hancock (Su-
    san the Silent), Keenan Wynn (Senator Rawkins), Al Freeman Jr. (Howard),
    Ronald Colby (Buzz Collins)
35 mm, 70 mm, color
141 min.

The Rain People (1969)
USA
Production: Warner Bros.–Seven Arts
Producers: Bart Patton and Ronald Colby (American Zoetrope)
Director: Francis Ford Coppola
Screenplay: Francis Ford Coppola
Photography: Bill Butler
Art Director: Leon Erickson
Editor: Barry Malkin
Music: Ronald Stein and Carmine Coppola
Sound: Nathan Boxer
Sound Montage: Walter Murch
Cast: James Caan (Kilgannon), Shirley Knight (Natalie Ravenna), Robert Duvall
    (Gordon), Marya Zimmet (Rosalie), Tom Aldredge (Mr. Alfred)
35 mm, color
101 min.

The Godfather (1972)
USA
Production: Paramount
Producer: Albert S. Ruddy

Director: Francis Ford Coppola
Screenplay: Mario Puzo and Francis Ford Coppola, based on the novel by
    Mario Puzo
Photography: Gordon Willis
Production Designer: Dean Tavoularis
Art Director: Warren Clymer
Costumes: Anna Hill Johnstone
Editors: William Reynolds and Peter Zinner
Music: Nino Rota, with additional music by Carmine Coppola
Sound: Christopher Newman
Cast: Marlon Brando (Vito Corleone), Al Pacino (Michael Corleone), James
    Caan (Sonny Corleone), Richard Castellano (Clemenza), Robert Duvall (Tom
    Hagen), Sterling Hayden (McCluskey), John Marley (Woltz), Richard Conte
    (Barzini), Al Lettieri (Sollozzo), Diane Keaton (Kay), Talia Shire (Connie),
    John Cazale (Fredo), Al Martino (Johnny Fontane)
35 mm, color
175 min.

The Conversation (1974)
USA
Production: Paramount
Producers: Francis Ford Coppola and Fred Roos (Directors Company)
Director: Francis Ford Coppola
Screenplay: Francis Ford Coppola
Photography: Bill Butler
Production Designer: Dean Tavoularis
Set Decorator: Doug von Koss
Costumes: Aggie Guerard Rodgers
Supervising Editor, Sound Montage, and Rerecording: Walter Murch
Editor: Richard Chew
Music: David Shire
Technical Advisers: Hal Lipset, Leo Jones, and Jim Bloom
Cast: Gene Hackman (Harry Caul), John Cazale (Stan), Allen Garfield (Bernie
    Moran), Frederic Forrest (Mark), Cindy Williams (Ann), Elizabeth McRae
    (Meredith), Harrison Ford (Martin Stett), Robert Duvall (the Director), Teri
    Garr (Amy)
35 mm, color
113 min.

The Godfather, Part II (1974)
USA
Production: Paramount
Producer: Francis Ford Coppola (American Zoetrope)

Director: Francis Ford Coppola
Screenplay: Francis Ford Coppola and Mario Puzo, based on events in the
   novel by Mario Puzo
Photography: Gordon Willis
Production Designer: Dean Tavoularis
Art Director: Angelo Graham
Set Decorator: George R. Neison
Costumes: Theadora van Runkle
Editors: Peter Zinner, Barry Malkin, and Richard Marks
Music: Nino Rota and Carmine Coppola
Sound Montage and Rerecording: Walter Murch
Cast: Al Pacino (Michael Corleone), Robert Duvall (Tom Hagen), Diane Keaton
   (Kay), Robert De Niro (Vito Corleone), John Cazale (Fredo Corleone), Talia
   Shire (Connie Corleone), Lee Strasberg (Hyman Roth), Michael V. Gazzo
   (Frank Pentangeli), G. D. Spradlin (Senator Pat Geary)
35 mm, color
200 min.

Apocalypse Now (1979)
USA
Production: United Artists
Producer: Francis Ford Coppola (American Zoetrope)
Director: Francis Ford Coppola
Screenplay: John Milius and Francis Ford Coppola, based on the novel *Heart
   of Darkness* by Joseph Conrad; Narration by Michael Herr
Photography: Vittorio Storaro
Production Designer: Dean Tavoularis
Art Director: Angelo Graham
Costume Supervisor: Charles E. James
Supervising Editor: Richard Marks
Editors: Walter Murch, Gerald B. Greenberg, Lisa Fruchtman, and Barry Malkin
Music: Carmine Coppola and Francis Ford Coppola
Sound Montage/Design: Walter Murch
Cast: Marlon Brando (Kurtz), Robert Duvall (Kilgore), Martin Sheen (Wil-
   lard), Frederic Forrest ("Chef"), Albert Hall (Chief), Sam Bottoms (Lance
   B. Johnson), Larry Fishburne ("Clean"), Dennis Hopper (Photojournalist),
   G. D. Spradlin (General Corman), Harrison Ford (Colonel Lucas)
35 mm, 70 mm, color
153 min.

One from the Heart (1982)
USA
Production: Columbia Pictures
Producers: Gray Frederickson and Fred Roos (Zoetrope Studios)

Director: Francis Ford Coppola
Screenplay: Armyan Bernstein and Francis Ford Coppola
Photography: Vittorio Storaro
Special Visual Effects: Robert Swarthe
Electronic Cinema: Thomas Brown, Murdo Laird, Anthony St. John, and Michael Lehmann
Production Designer: Dean Tavoularis
Art Director: Angelo Graham
Costumes: Ruth Morley
Choreographers: Kenny Ortega and Gene Kelly
Editors: Anne Goursaud, with Rudi Fehr and Randy Roberts
Songs and Music: Tom Waits; Performed by Tom Waits and Crystal Gayle
Sound Designer: Richard Beggs
Cast: Frederic Forrest (Hank), Teri Garr (Frannie), Raul Julia (Ray), Nastassia Kinski (Leila), Lainie Kazan (Maggie), Harry Dean Stanton (Moe)
35 mm, 70 mm, color
107 min.

The Outsiders (1983)
USA
Production: Warner Bros.
Producers: Fred Roos and Gray Frederickson (Zoetrope Studios)
Director: Francis Ford Coppola
Screenplay: S. E. Hinton and Francis Ford Coppola, based on the novel by S. E. Hinton
Photography: Steven H. Burum
Special Visual Effects: Robert Swarthe
Production Designer: Dean Tavoularis
Costumes: Marge Bowers
Editor: Anne Goursaud
Music: Carmine Coppola
Sound: Jim Webb
Sound Designer: Richard Beggs
Cast: Matt Dillon (Dallas Winston), Ralph Macchio (Johnny Cade), C. Thomas Howell (Ponyboy Curtis), Patrick Swayze (Darrel Curtis), Rob Lowe (Sodapop Curtis), Emilio Estevez (Two-Bit Matthews), Tom Cruise (Steve Randle), Glenn Withrow (Tom Shepard), Diane Lane (Cherry Valance), Tom Waits (Buck Merrill)
35 mm, color
91 min.

Rumble Fish (1983)
USA
Production: Universal

Producers: Fred Roos and Doug Claybourne (Zoetrope Studios)
Director: Francis Ford Coppola
Screenplay: S. E. Hinton and Francis Ford Coppola, based on the novel by
S. E. Hinton
Photography: Steven H. Burum
Production Designer: Dean Tavoularis
Costumes: Marge Bowers
Editor: Barry Malkin
Music: Stewart Copeland
Sound: David Parker
Sound Designer: Richard Beggs
Cast: Matt Dillon (Rusty James), Mickey Rourke (Motorcycle Boy), Diane Lane
(Patty), Dennis Hopper (Father), Diane Scarwid (Cassandra), Vincent Spano
(Steve), Nicolas Cage (Smokey), Christopher Penn (B. J. Jackson), Larry
Fishburne (Midget), William Smith (Patterson), Tom Waits (Benny)
35 mm, black and white
94 min.

The Cotton Club (1984)
USA
Production: Orion
Producer: Robert Evans (Zoetrope Studios)
Director: Francis Ford Coppola
Screenplay: William Kennedy and Francis Ford Coppola, from a story by William Kennedy
Photography: Stephen Goldblatt
Production Designer: Richard Sylbert
Art Directors: David Chapman and Gregory Bolton
Costumes: Milena Canonero
Principal Choreographer: Michael Smith
Tap Choreographer: Henry LeTang
Sound Editor: Edward Beyer
Montage and Second-Unit Director: Gian-Carlo Coppola
Editor: Barry Malkin
Music: John Barry and Bob Wilber
Cast: Richard Gere (Dixie Dwyer), Gregory Hines (Sandman Williams), Diane
Lane (Vera Cicero), Lonette McKee (Lila Rose Oliver), Bob Hoskins (Owney
Madden), James Remar (Dutch Schultz), Nicolas Cage (Vincent Dwyer)
35 mm, 70 mm, color
127 min.

Peggy Sue Got Married (1986)
USA
Production: Tri-Star

Producer: Paul R. Gurian (American Zoetrope)
Director: Francis Ford Coppola
Screenplay: Jerry Leichtling and Arlene Sarner
Photography: Jordan Cronenweth
Electronic Cinema: Murdo Laird, Ted Mackland, and Ron Mooreland
Production Designer: Dean Tavoularis
Art Designer: Alex Tavoularis
Costumes: Theadora Van Runkle
Editor: Barry Malkin
Music: John Barry
Supervisory Sound Editor: Michael Kirchberger
Cast: Kathleen Turner (Peggy Sue Kelcher), Nicolas Cage (Charlie Bodell), Barry
    Miller (Richard Norvik), Catherine Hicks (Carol Heath), Joan Allen (Maddie
    Nagel), Kevin J. O'Connor (Michael Fitzsimmons), Jim Carrey (Walter Getz)
35 mm, color
104 min.

Gardens of Stone (1987)
USA
Production: Tri-Star
Producers: Michael I. Levy and Francis Ford Coppola
Director: Francis Ford Coppola
Screenplay: Ronald Bass, based on the novel by Nicholas Proffitt
Photography: Jordan Cronenweth
Production Designer: Dean Tavoularis
Art Designer: Alex Tavoularis
Costumes: Will Kim and Judianna Makovsky
Editor: Barry Malkin
Music: Carmine Coppola
Sound Designer: Richard Beggs
Cast: James Caan (Clell Hazard), Anjelica Huston (Samantha Davis), James
    Earl Jones (Sgt. Maj. Goody Nelson), D. B. Sweeney (Jackie Willow), Dean
    Stockwell (Homer Thomas), Mary Stuart Masterson (Rachel Feld)
35 mm, color
111 min.   .

Tucker: The Man and His Dream (1989)
USA
Production: Paramount
Producers: Fred Roos and Fred Fuchs (Lucasfilm Ltd. and Zoetrope Studios)
Director: Francis Ford Coppola
Screenplay: Arnold Schulman and David Seidler
Photography: Vittorio Storaro
Production Designer: Dean Tavoularis

Art Director: Alex Tavoularis
Costumes: Milena Canonero
Editor: Priscilla Nedd
Music: Joe Jackson
Sound Designer: Richard Beggs
Cast: Jeff Bridges (Preston Tucker), Joan Allen (Vera), Martin Landau (Abe
    Karatz), Frederic Forrest (Eddie), Mako (Jimmy), Elias Koteas (Alex), Chris-
    tian Slater (Junior)
35 mm, color
110 min.

New York Stories (Segment: *Life without Zoe* [1989])
USA
Production: Touchstone Pictures
Producers: Fred Roos and Fred Fuchs
Director: Francis Ford Coppola
Screenplay: Francis Ford Coppola and Sofia Coppola
Photography: Vittorio Storaro
Production Designer: Dean Tavoularis
Art Director: Speed Hopkins
Costumes: Sofia Coppola
Editor: Barry Malkin
Music: Carmine Coppola
Sound Recording: Frank Graziadei
Songs: Kid Creole and the Coconuts
Cast: Heather McComb (Zoe), Talia Shire (Charlotte), Gia Coppola (Baby Zoe),
    Giancarlo Giannini (Claudio), Paul Herman (Clifford)
35 mm, color
34 min.

The Godfather, Part III (1990)
USA
Production: Paramount
Producer: Francis Ford Coppola (Zoetrope Studios)
Director: Francis Ford Coppola
Screenplay: Mario Puzo and Francis Ford Coppola
Photography: Gordon Willis
Production Designer: Dean Tavoularis
Art Director: Alex Tavoularis
Costumes: Milena Canonero
Editors: Barry Malkin, Lisa Fruchtman, and Walter Murch
Music: Carmine Coppola
Additional Music and Themes: Nino Rota
Sound Designer: Richard Beggs

Cast: Al Pacino (Michael Corleone), Diane Keaton (Kay), Talia Shire (Connie Corleone), Andy Garcia (Vincent Mancini), Eli Wallach (Don Altobello), Joe Mantegna (Joey Zasa), George Hamilton (B. J. Harrison), Bridget Fonda (Grace Hamilton), Sofia Coppola (Mary Corleone), Franc D'Ambrosio (Anthony Corleone)
35 mm, color
170 min.

Bram Stoker's Dracula (1992)
USA
Production: Columbia Pictures
Producers: Francis Ford Coppola, Fred Fuchs, and Charles Mulvehill (American Zoetrope)
Director: Francis Ford Coppola
Screenplay: James V. Hart
Photography: Michael Ballhaus
Visual Effects: Roman Coppola
Production Designer: Thomas Sanders
Art Director: Andrew Precht
Costumes: Eiko Ishioka
Editors: Nicholas C. Smith, Glenn Scantlebury, and Anne Goursaud
Music: Wojciech Kilar
Sound: David Stone
Cast: Gary Oldman (Dracula), Winona Ryder (Mina/Elisabeta), Anthony Hopkins (Van Helsing), Keanu Reeves (Jonathan Harker), Sadie Frost (Lucy Westenra), Richard E. Grant (Dr. Jack Seward), Cary Elwes (Arthur Holmwood), Tom Waits (Renfield)
35 mm, color
128 min.

Jack (1996)
USA
Production: Buena Vista
Producers: Ricardo Mestres, Fred Fuchs, and Francis Ford Coppola (American Zoetrope)
Director: Francis Ford Coppola
Screenplay: James DeMonaco and Gary Nadeau
Photography: John Toll
Production Designer: Dean Tavoularis
Art Designer: Angelo Graham
Costumes: Aggie Guerard Rodgers
Editor: Barry Malkin
Music: Michael Kamen
Sound: Agamemnon Andrianos

Cast: Robin Williams (Jack Powell), Diane Lane (Karen Powell), Jennifer Lopez (Miss Marquez), Brian Kerwin (Brian Powell), Fran Drescher (Dolores Durante), Bill Cosby (Lawrence Woodruff), Michael McKean (Paulie)
35 mm, color
113 min.

The Rainmaker (1997)
USA
Production: Paramount
Producers: Michael Douglas, Steven Reuther, and Fred Fuchs (American Zoetrope)
Director: Francis Ford Coppola
Screenplay: Francis Ford Coppola, based on the novel by John Grisham
Photography: John Toll
Production Designer: Howard Cummings
Art Directors: Robert Shaw and Jeffrey McDonald
Costumes: Aggie Guerard Rodgers
Editor: Barry Malkin
Music: Elmer Bernstein
Sound: Nelson Stoll
Cast: Matt Damon (Rudy Baylor), Claire Danes (Kelly Riker), Jon Voight (Leo F. Drummond), Mary Kay Place (Dot Black), Mickey Rourke (Bruiser Stone), Danny DeVito (Deck Schifflet), Dean Stockwell (Judge Harvey Hale), Teresa Wright (Miss Birdie), Virginia Madsen (Jackie Lemancyzk)
35 mm, color
135 min.

Youth without Youth (2007)
USA
Production: American Zoetrope
Producer: Francis Ford Coppola
Director: Francis Ford Coppola
Screenplay: Francis Ford Coppola, based on the novella by Mircea Eliade
Photography: Mihai Malaimare Jr.
Production Designer: Calin Papura
Editor: Walter Murch
Music: Osvaldo Golijov
Cast: Tim Roth (Dominic), Alexandra Maria Lara (Veronica/Laura), Bruno Ganz (Professor Stanciulescu), André Hennicke (Josef Rudolf)
35 mm, color
124 min.

Tetro (2009)
USA

Production: American Zoetrope
Producer: Francis Ford Coppola
Director: Francis Ford Coppola
Screenplay: Francis Ford Coppola
Photography: Mihai Malaimare Jr.
Production Designer: Sebastián Orgambide
Art Designer: Federico García Cambero
Editor: Walter Murch
Music: Osvaldo Golijov
Cast: Vincent Gallo (Angelo "Tetro" Tetrocini), Alden Ehrenreich (Bennie),
Maribel Verdú (Miranda), Carmen Maura (Alone)
35 min, black and white
127 min.

Twixt (2011)
USA
Production: American Zoetrope
Producer: Francis Ford Coppola
Director: Francis Ford Coppola
Screenplay: Francis Ford Coppola
Photography: Mihai Malaimare Jr.
Art Director: Jimmy DiMarcellis
Editor: Robert Schafer
Music: Osvaldo Golijov and Dan Deacon
Cast: Val Kilmer (Hall Baltimore), Bruce Dern (Sheriff Bobby LaGrange), Elle
Fanning (V), Ben Chaplin (Poe), Joanne Whalley (Denise), David Paymer
(Sam), Alden Ehrenreich (Flamingo)
35 mm, color
88 min.

Arrighi, Giovanni. *The Long Twentieth Century*. London: Verso, 1994.

Bart, Peter. "Three's 'Company.'" *Variety*, December 6, 2004, 68. Coppola files, Pacific Film Archive, Berkeley, Calif.

Baumann, Shyon. *Hollywood Highbrow*. Princeton, N.J.: Princeton University Press, 2007.

Bolter, Jay David, and Richard Grusin. *Remediation*. Cambridge: Massachusetts Institute of Technology Press, 1999.

Bordwell, David, Janet Staiger, and Kristin Thompson. *The Classical Hollywood Cinema*. New York: Columbia University Press, 1985.

Carver, Benedict. "New Dreams for Zoetrope." *Variety*, July 20, 1998, 7, 10.

Castells, Manuel, and Alejandro Portes. "World Underneath: The Origins, Dynamics, and Effects of the Informal Economy." In *The Informal Economy*. Ed. Alejandro Portes, Manuel Castells, and Lauren A. Benton. Baltimore: Johns Hopkins University Press, 1989. 11–40.

Cavell, Stanley. *The World Viewed*. Cambridge, Mass.: Harvard University Press, 1979.

Chandler, Alfred D., Jr. *Scale and Scope: The Dynamics of Industrial Capitalism*. Cambridge, Mass.: Harvard University Press, 1990.

Coase, Ronald. "The Nature of the Firm." In *The Nature of the Firm*. Ed. Oliver E. Williamson and Sidney G. Winter. New York: Oxford University Press, 1991. 18–33.

Connor, J. D. *The Studios after the Studios: Neoclassical Hollywood, 1970–2010*. Stanford, Calif.: Stanford University Press, forthcoming.

Coppola, Eleanor. *Notes*. New York: Limelight Editions, 2001.

———. *Notes on a Life*. New York: Doubleday, 2008.

Cook, David A. *History of the American Cinema*. Vol. 9: *Lost Illusions: American Cinema in the Shadow of Watergate and Vietnam, 1970–1970*. New York: Charles Scribner's Sons, 2000.

Corliss, Richard. "Coppola's *Tetro*: An Offer You Can Refuse." *Time*, June 11, 2009; accessed February 20, 2014. http://content.time.com/time/arts/article/0,8599,1904079,00.html.

Cowie, Peter. *Coppola.* New York: Da Capo Press, 1994.

Cutts, John. "The Dangerous Age." *Films and Filming* (May 1969): 4–10. Coppola files, Pacific Film Archive, Berkeley, Calif.

Deleuze, Gilles. *Cinema 1: The Movement-Image.* Trans. Hugh Tomlinson and Barbara Habberjam. Minneapolis: University of Minnesota Press, 1986.

Dellheim, Charles. "The Creation of a Company Culture." *American Historical Review* 92.1 (February 1987): 13–44.

Drucker, Peter F. "Henry Ford: Success and Failure." *Harper's Magazine* 195.116 (July 1947): 1–8.

———. *The Practice of Management.* New York: Harper and Row, 1954.

Eugenides, Jeffrey. *The Virgin Suicides.* New York: Picador, 1993.

Friedan, Betty. *The Feminine Mystique.* New York: W. W. Norton and Co., 1997.

Glyn, Andrew. *Capitalism Unleashed.* Oxford: Oxford University Press, 2006.

Grantham, Bill. "Embracing Jurisdiction: John Ford's *The Man Who Shot Liberty Valance.*" In *Jurisprudence of Jurisdiction.* Ed. Shaun McVeigh. New York: Routledge-Cavendish, 2007. 225–37.

Handy, Bruce. "The Liberation of Francis Ford Coppola." *Vanity Fair* (December 2007); accessed April 9, 2014. http://www.vanityfair.com/culture/features/2007/12/coppola200712.

Hansen, Miriam. "Traces of Transgression in *Apocalypse Now.*" *Social Text* 3 (Autumn 1980): 123–35.

Harvey, David. *The Condition of Postmodernity.* Oxford: Wiley-Blackwell, 1991.

Hayden, Tom. *The Port Huron Statement: The Visionary Call of the 1960s Revolution.* New York: Thunder's Mouth Press, 2005.

Hegel, G. W. F. *Philosophy of Right.* Trans. T. M. Knox. London: Oxford University Press, 1967.

Horowitz, Daniel. *Betty Friedan and the Making of* The Feminine Mystique*: The American Left, the Cold War, and Modern Feminism.* Amherst: University of Massachusetts Press, 1998.

Jameson, Fredric. "The Brick and the Balloon." In *The Cultural Turn: Selected Writings on the Postmodern, 1983–1998.* London: Verso, 1998. 162–89.

———. "Reification and Utopia in Mass Culture." In *Signatures of the Visible.* New York: Routledge, 1992. 9–34.

Kael, Pauline. *Raising Kane.* London: Methuen Publishing, 2002.

Klawans, Stuart. "Tucker: The Man and His Dream." *The Nation* 247.7 (September 26, 1988): 250.

Kline, Sally, ed. *George Lucas Interviews.* Jackson: University Press of Mississippi, 1999.

Koss, Juliet. *Modernism after Wagner.* Minneapolis: University of Minnesota Press, 2010.

Lash, Scott, and John Urry. *The End of Organized Capitalism.* Madison: University of Wisconsin Press, 1987.

Lee, Nathan. "Pretty Vacant." *Film Comment* 42.5 (September 1, 2006): 24–26.

Lewis, Jon. *The Godfather.* London: Palgrave Macmillan, 2010.

———. "The Perfect Money Machine(s): George Lucas, Steven Spielberg, and Auteurism in the New Hollywood." In *Looking Past the Screen.* Ed. Jon Lewis and Eric Smoodin. Durham, N.C.: Duke University Press, 2007. 61–86.

———. *Whom God Wishes to Destroy.* Durham, N.C.: Duke University Press, 1996.

Lindsey, Robert. "Francis Ford Coppola: Promises to Keep." *New York Times Magazine,* July 24, 1988, 23–27.

Lyotard, Jean-François. *The Postmodern Condition.* Trans. Geoff Bennington and Brian Massumi. Minneapolis: University of Minnesota Press, 1993.

Machen, Arthur. "Corporate Personality." *Harvard Law Review* 24.4 (1911): 253–67.

Marcus, Greil. "Journeying Up the River: An Interview with Francis Ford Coppola." *Rolling Stone,* November 1, 1979, 51–57.

McGregor, Douglas. "The Human Side of Enterprise." *Management Review* 46.1 (1957): 22–28.

Miller, D. A. *Place for Us: Essay on the Broadway Musical.* Cambridge, Mass.: Harvard University Press, 1998.

Miller, Toby, Nitin Govil, John McMurria, Ting Wang, and Richard Maxwell. *Global Hollywood 2.* London: British Film Institute Publishing, 2005.

Monson, Karen. "Coppola Directs American Premier of 'The Visit.'" *Los Angeles Herald-Examiner,* October 31, 1972, C-4.

Motley, Bob. "Two 'Godfathers' Are Better than One." *New Times,* May 3, 1974, 58–59.

Nachman, Gerald. "Coppola of Zoetrope—Older, Wiser, and Poorer." *Los Angeles Times,* November 7, 1971, 57.

Nagel, Ivan. *Autonomy and Mercy.* Cambridge, Mass.: Harvard University Press, 1991.

Nietzsche, Friedrich. *The Birth of Tragedy and the Case of Wagner.* Trans. Walter Kaufmann. New York: Vintage, 1967.

Nilges, Mathias. "The Anti-Anti-Oedipus: Representing Post-Fordist Subjectivity." *Mediations* 23.2 (Spring 2008): 26–69.

Offe, Claus. *Disorganized Capitalism.* Cambridge: Massachusetts Institute of Technology Press, 1985.

Ondaatje, Michael. *The Conversations.* New York: Knopf, 2002.

Parisi, Paula. "A Conversation with Francis Ford Coppola." *American Cinematographer* 72.8 (August 1991): 71–73.

Phillips, Gene D. *Godfather.* Lexington: University Press of Kentucky, 2004.

Phillips, Gene D., and Rodney Hill, eds. *Francis Ford Coppola Interviews.* Jackson: University Press of Mississippi, 2004.

Potter, Paul. "We Must Name the System." In *The Sixties Papers: Documents of a Rebellious Decade.* Ed. Judith Clavier Albert and Stewart Edward Albert. New York: Praeger, 1984. 218–25.

Pye, Michael and Lynda Myles. *The Movie Brats: How the Film Generation Took Over Hollywood.* New York: Holt, Rinehart, and Winston, 1979.

Rafferty, Terrence. "Tucker: The Man and His Dream." *New Yorker* 64.27 (August 22, 1988): 62.

Rohter, Larry. "Family Dynamics, without the Bullets." *New York Times,* June 3, 2009; accessed February 24, 2014. www.nytimes.com/2009/06/07/movies/07roht.html?_r=0.

Rubin, Harriet. "Art of Darkness." *Fast Company* 18 (October 1998): 134–37.

Sarris, Andrew. *The American Cinema: Directors and Directions, 1929–1968.* New York: E. P. Dutton and Co., 1968.

Sartre, Jean-Paul. *What Is Literature?* Trans. Bernard Frechtman. London: Routledge, 2001.

Schaefer, Dennis, and Larry Salvato. *Masters of Light.* Berkeley: University of California Press, 1985.

Schatz, Thomas. *The Genius of the System.* Minneapolis: University of Minnesota Press, 2010.

Scheer, Robert, and Susan Lyne. "An Interview with Francis Ford Coppola." *City of San Francisco,* December 2, 1975, 22.

Schumacher, Michael. *Francis Ford Coppola.* New York: Crown Publishers, 1999.

"S.F. Film Craft Union Gives Coppola Full Control in Return for 55-Hr. Week." *Variety,* September 24, 1969, 22. Coppola files, Pacific Film Archive, Berkeley, Calif.

Simons, Dan. "Francis Ford Coppola and American Zoetrope." *Entertainment World,* March 27, 1970, 15–17. Coppola files, Pacific Film Archive, Berkeley, Calif.

———. "'Rain People' by Rule Breaker." *Los Angeles Times,* September 9, 1969, 1.

Smith, Christopher, John Child, and Michael Rowlinson. *Reshaping Work: The Cadbury Experience.* Cambridge: Cambridge University Press, 1990.

Smith, Murray. "Theses on the Philosophy of Hollywood History." In *Contemporary Hollywood Cinema.* Ed. Steve Neale and Murray Smith. London: Routledge, 1998. 3–20.

Sweeney, Louise. "The Movie Business Is Alive and Well and Living in San Francisco." *Show* 1 (April 1970): 34–37, 82.

Ventura, Michael. "Coppola's Woes and the Zoetrope Revolution." *L.A. Weekly,* February 13, 1981, 7–10.

Wasko, Janet. *Movies and Money.* Norwood, N.J.: Ablex Publishing, 1982.

Žižek, Slavoj. *Tarrying with the Negative.* Durham, N.C.: Duke University Press, 1993.

Index

Adorno, Theodor W., 89
Air (rock band), 110
Alexander Nevsky, 95
American Graffiti, 19–20
American in Paris, An, 103
American Zoetrope: as business idea, 3–4,
    9, 20–21; facility, 39–40; and financial
    crisis, 43; formation, 23–27; work con-
    ditions, 15, 37–39
Antonioni, Michelangelo, 30, 65–66
Apartment, The, 65
Apocalypse Now, 18, 21, 23, 43–44, 67,
    76–78, 82–90, 93, 104
Arizona Dream, 97
Arrighi, Giovanni, 18
Ashley, Ted, 40, 43, 44
Ashley-Famous, 44
Astaire, Fred, 25
Auteur Theory, 2, 7–9

Bach, Steven, 1
Bart, Peter, 60
BBS Productions, 58
Beatles, The, 101
Beggs, Richard, 73
Bergson, Henri, 35
Bernstein, Leonard, 16
Bizet, George, 80
Blow-Up, 65–66
Bluhdorn, Charles, 23, 60
Bogdanovich, Peter, 60, 67
Bohème, La, 78
Bolter, Jay David, 74
Bram Stoker's Dracula, 22

Brand, Stewart, 13
Brando, Marlon, 54, 82
Braudel, Fernand, 17
Bridges, Jeff, 4
business management: under Fordism,
    11–12; managerialism, 44–45 scientific
    management, 2, 8, 11, 65
Butler, Bill, 29

Caan, James, 29, 33
Cadbury Brothers, Ltd., 58
Calley, John, 40, 43, 44
Camelot, 25
Capra, Frank, 4, 16, 69–70
Carnegie, Andrew, 69
Carmen, 80
Carmichael, Stokely, 25
Cassavetes, John, 95–96
Castells, Manuel, 6
Cavalleria Rusticana, 92, 94, 100
Cavell, Stanley, 105
Cazale, John, 61
Cecilia Valdés, 78
Chandler, Alfred D., Jr., 44, 57
Chaplin, Charlie, 2
Chion, Michel, 77
Citizen Kane, 9
Coase, Ronald, 56, 89
Colby, Ronald, 25, 40
Comden, Betty, 16, 101
Connor, J. D., 72
Conversation, The, 23, 29, 42, 43, 45, 51,
    59–67
Coppola, Anton, 98

Coppola, August, 77
Coppola, Carmine, 12, 77–78, 86, 98
Coppola, Eleanor, 40, 78, 85
Coppola, Francis Ford: awards, 24,
    67; childhood, 12, 78, 86; economic
    change, 3, 7, 12–19; film school, 3, 9,
    24, 27; technology, 17, 38–39, 83–84,
    102–3, 104–6; wine-making, 96
Coppola, Roman, 23, 107, 111
Coppola, Sofia, 23, 91, 96, 101–4, 107–11
Corliss, Richard, 98
Corman, Roger, 3, 23, 86
corporation: and conglomerates, 3, 23–24
    44–45, 57, 94, 96, 111; incorporation of
    American Zoetrope, 40; and opera, 22,
    78–79; personal firms, 57–58; theory
    of, 56–57, 81–82
Costello, Elvis, 100–101, 108
Cotton Club, The, 22
Cowie, Peter, 28, 30, 33, 34
Cuba, 59, 77

Daisy Miller, 60
D'Ambrosio, Franc, 90
Deleuze, Gilles, 35–36
Dementia 13, 9, 38
Denby, David, 102
Deschanel, Caleb, 23
Director's Company, 51, 59, 67, 88
Disney Company, 58
Douglas, Michael, 49
Drucker, Peter, 14–15
Dunst, Kirsten, 108
Duvall, Robert, 28–29, 33, 82, 85

Easy Rider, 3
Edison, Thomas, 9, 16, 69
Ehrenreich, Alden, 97
Einem, Gottfried von, 78
Eugenides, Jeffrey, 108
Evans, Robert, 54
Exorcist, The, 60

Feminine Mystique, The, 27
Filmmaker, 37–38
Finian's Rainbow, 9, 23, 25, 38, 101
Fishburne, Laurence, 83
Flivver King, The, 32

Ford, Harrison, 86
Ford, Henry, 9–14, 16, 32
Ford, John, 10–12
Forrest, Frederic, 103
Free Speech Movement, 47
French Connection, The, 67
Friedan, Betty, 12, 27–28, 36
Friedkin, William, 60, 67
Friedman, Milton, 12

Gallo, Vincent, 97
Gang of Four, 108
Garcia, Andy, 91
Garcia, Jerry, 3, 40
Gardens of Stone, 68
Garr, Teri, 62, 103
Gecko, Gordon, 49
Gesamtkuntswerk, 81
Gluck, Christoph Willibald, 79
Godfather, The, 4, 7, 9, 23, 42–59, 64, 77,
    78, 89, 90, 93, 97, 98, 102
Godfather, Part II, 48, 58–59, 67, 97, 101
Godfather, Part III, 23, 42, 76–77, 90–95,
    99, 100
Godfather trilogy, 1, 28–30, 58, 61, 90,
    93, 95, 97, 98, 100–103
Good Machine, 94
Graduate, The, 49, 111
Graham, Bill, 3, 40
Green, Adolph, 16, 101
Griffith, D. W., 2
Grover-Friedlander, Michal, 77, 89
Grusin, Richard, 74
Guatarri, Félix, 36
Gulf and Western, 23, 60

Hackman, Gene, 61
Hansen, Miriam, 21, 76, 83, 85
Hard Day's Night, A, 111
Harvey, David, 12
Hegel, G. W. F., 57–59, 92
Herzog, Werner, 77
His Girl Friday, 65
Hole in the Head, A, 70
Holly, Buddy, 101
Hollywood General, 16, 102, 103
Hopper, Dennis, 3, 87
Horowitz, Daniel, 28

How Green Was My Valley, 12
Hyman, Kenny, 27

I Am Curious Yellow, 40
Industrial Light and Magic, 106
It's a Wonderful Life, 70
Ivens, Joris, 35

James, Henry, 60
Jameson, Fredric, 57, 104, 105
Jobs, Steve, 12
Jonze, Spike, 111
Juliá, Raúl, 104

Kael, Pauline, 9
Kaufman, Richard, 49
Kazan, Lainie, 106
Keaton, Diane, 48
Kerkorian, Kirk, 23
Kelly, Gene, 103–5
Kerman, Joseph, 79
Kesey, Ken, 40
Kinney National Services, Inc., 25, 40
Kinski, Nastassja, 105
Klawans, Stuart, 72, 98
Korty, John, 1, 19
Knight, Shirley, 30
Kreilkamp, Ivan, 86
Kusturica, Emir, 97

Landau, Martin, 8, 73
Last Picture Show, The, 60
L'Avventura, 30
Lee, Nathan, 109
Les contes d'Hoffman, 99
Lester, Richard, 25
Lewis, Jon, 49, 60, 69–70, 75, 98, 102
Liberal Consensus, 7, 46–47
Life without Zoe, 98
Lindsey, Robert, 69, 71
Lloyd, Harold, 103
Lohengrin, 80
Lost in Translation, 108
Lovin' Spoonful, 111
Lucas, George, 1, 4, 18, 19–21, 24–28,
    37–40, 43, 44, 51, 68–74, 86, 106
Lucasfilm, 16, 68, 72–73
Lumet, Sidney, 93

Macdonald, Dwight, 2
Malkin, Barry, 28
Mann, Michael, 93
Marcus, Greil, 84
Marie Antoinette, 23, 102, 108–10
Marley, John, 50
Mascagni, Pietro, 94, 100
Megalopolis, 14–17
MGM, 23, 101, 104, 110
Milius, John, 3, 7
Miller, D. A., 105
Modern Times, 2
Monteverdi, Claudio, 79
Mozart, Wolgang Amadeus, 79–80
Mr. Deeds Goes to Town, 70
Mr. Smith Goes to Washington, 70
Murch, Walter, 1, 3, 24, 25, 39, 98
Murray, Bill, 108
My Aim Is True, 101

Nagel, Ivan, 79
"Natural's Not in It," 108
Nerab, Jack, 70
New Economy, 3, 17–18, 41
New Left, 17, 49
Nietzsche, Friedrich, 80–82
Nilges, Mathias, 32

October Films, 94
Offenbach, Jacques, 99
Oglesby, Carl, 49
One from the Heart, 16, 23, 52, 67, 76,
    85, 93, 101–7, 110, 111
Opera: and cinema, 76–78; and the corporation, 21–22, 78–82; and modernity,
    78–81; and the musical, 100–104; Orpheus and Eurydice, 79, 89
Outsiders, The, 22

Pacino, Al, 4
Paramount, 43, 60, 95
Patton, 38, 45–47
Patton, Bart, 37
Peggy Sue Got Married, 68, 71, 105
Phoenix (rock band), 110
Portes, Alejandro, 6
Port Huron Statement, 17, 24, 39
Powell, Michael, 77, 99, 103

Pressburger, Emeric, 77, 99
Prince, Stephen, 106
Puzo, Mario, 43

Radley, Gordon, 71
Rafferty, Terrence, 73, 75
Raging Bull, 94, 100
Rain, 35
Rain People, The, 9, 18, 23–43, 59, 88
Renoir, Jean, 35
"Ride of the Valkyries," 82–83
Rock around the Clock, 111
Rohter, Larry, 97
Rossman, Michael, 47
Rota, Nino, 53
Rumble Fish, 52, 105

Sarris, Andrew, 7
Sartre, Jean-Paul, 81, 87
Schopenhauer, Arthur, 82
Schumacher, Michael, 60
Schumpeter, Joseph, 36
Scorsese, Martin, 77, 93, 94, 100
Sheen, Martin, 82
Simons, Dan, 37
Sinclair, Upton, 32
Singer, Jack, 93
Sjöman, Vilgot, 39
Skot-Hansen, Mogens, 39–40, 58, 88
Sloan, Alfred, 45
Somewhere, 110
Spielberg, Steven, 71
Stagecoach, 12
Staiger, Janet, 11, 45
Stanton, Harry Dean, 106
Star Wars, 44, 68, 74
Storaro, Vittorio, 104
Strasberg, Lee, 101, 103
Stroheim, Erich von, 2
Strokes, the, 109

Students for a Democratic Society (SDS), 24
Syberberg, Hans-Jürgen, 77

Tales of Hoffman, The, 99
Technicolor, 100, 104–5
Tetro, 23, 76–77, 90, 96–100
Thalberg, Irving, 2
Thompson, David, 49
THX-1138, 16, 19–21, 23, 38, 43
Towne, Robert, 52
Tucker, 4–10, 14, 15–16, 23, 29, 45, 51, 67–76, 101
Tucker, Preston, 29, 40
Turner, Fred, 3

Vanderbeek, Stan, 19
Verdi, Giuseppe, 89, 90
Virgin Suicides, The, 23, 96, 102, 108
Visconti, Luchino, 77
Visit of the Old Lady, 78
Vocal Apparitions, 77

Wagner, Richard, 80–83, 89, 90
Waits, Tom, 103, 107
Wall Street, 49
Warner, Jack, 25
Warner Bros., 3, 16, 24, 40, 43–45, 96
Warner-Seven Arts merger, 25
Welles, Orson, 9, 60
Whom God Wishes to Destroy, 102
Why We Fight, 70

Yablans, Frank, 60
You're a Big Boy Now, 9, 23, 25, 38, 111
Youth without Youth, 96

Zanuck, Darryl, 105
Zitelman, Ernst, 81
Žižek, Slavoj, 91–92

Jeff Menne is an assistant professor of screen studies and English at Oklahoma State University.

Books in the series Contemporary Film Directors

Nelson Pereira dos Santos
Darlene J. Sadlier

Abbas Kiarostami
Mehrnaz Saeed-Vafa and Jonathan Rosenbaum

Joel and Ethan Coen
R. Barton Palmer

Claire Denis
Judith Mayne

Wong Kar-wai
Peter Brunette

Edward Yang
John Anderson

Pedro Almodóvar
Marvin D'Lugo

Chris Marker
Nora Alter

Abel Ferrara
Nicole Brenez, translated by Adrian Martin

Jane Campion
Kathleen McHugh

Jim Jarmusch
Juan Suárez

Roman Polanski
James Morrison

Manoel de Oliveira
John Randal Johnson

Neil Jordan
Maria Pramaggiore

Paul Schrader
George Kouvaros

Jean-Pierre Jeunet
Elizabeth Ezra

Terrence Malick
Lloyd Michaels

Sally Potter
Catherine Fowler

Atom Egoyan
Emma Wilson

Albert Maysles
Joe McElhaney

Jerry Lewis
Chris Fujiwara

Jean-Pierre and Luc Dardenne
Joseph Mai

Michael Haneke
Peter Brunette

Alejandro González Iñárritu
Celestino Deleyto and Maria del Mar Azcona

Lars von Trier
Linda Badley

Hal Hartley
Mark L. Berrettini

François Ozon
Thibaut Schilt

Steven Soderbergh
Aaron Baker

Mike Leigh
Sean O'Sullivan

D.A. Pennebaker
Keith Beattie

Jacques Rivette
Mary M. Wiles

Kim Ki-duk
Hye Seung Chung

Philip Kaufman
Annette Insdorf

Richard Linklater
David T. Johnson

David Lynch
Justus Nieland

John Sayles
David R. Shumway

Dario Argento
L. Andrew Cooper

Todd Haynes
Rob White

Christian Petzold
Jaimey Fisher

Spike Lee
Todd McGowan

Terence Davies
Michael Koresky

Francis Ford Coppola
Jeff Menne